D1520301

1

The Systems Thinker – Mental Models

Take Control Over Your Thought Patterns.
Learn Advanced Decision-Making and Problem-
Solving Skills.

By Albert Rutherford

of further information does not mean that the author endorses the information the individual, organization to website may provide or recommendations they/it may make. Further, readers should be aware that Internet websites listed in this work might have changed or disappeared between when this work was written and when it is read.

For general information on the products and services or to obtain technical support, please contact the author.

ISBN: 9798862303421

www.albertrutherford.com

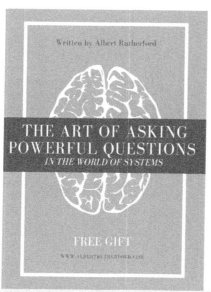

To get your Free Gift, The Art of Asking Powerful Questions in the World of Systems, visit www.albertrutherford.com

Table of Contents

Introduction

Systems thinking is a fascinating thinking tool that expands our cognitive horizons if used well. However, what "well" means and what people understand under the aegis of "thinking in systems" may vary. This cognitive method stretches beyond simple rules. People who become interested in learning about systems are usually fascinated by the complex diagrams—like causal loop diagrams—or other management simulation tools provided by systems thinking. They think that, by learning to use the tools, it will help them fix their problems.

But systems thinking isn't only theoretical knowledge—it has a strong connection to the events that have happened and are currently happening in our world. Whatever happens in the world has a cause and an effect, and this effect can spill over and create some unintended consequences. Other events have a circular nature that feed back to the structures responsible in creating them. There can be blind spots and powerfully influencing laws in the systems we are

13

not cognizant of. We can also be totally unaware of some of our own contributions to a negative or positive change.

For example, if we make a mistake and we are treated with blame instead of understanding and a genuine intent to right our wrongs, we become rather defensive. We close our minds off from learning opportunities in our self-righteousness, thus we don't improve, and we become even more prone to making errors. We enter a vicious cycle of blame and error. What's the way out? You'll learn in this book.

Systems thinking done well, therefore, is more than learning to use a model. It's a knowledge thanks to which we understand and comprehensively see complex phenomena by using models, while expanding our awareness to the interconnectedness of the problem we're analyzing.

We can use systems thinking to diagnose problems just like a good doctor following the analysis-diagnosis-solution trio. We first take a look at the problem at hand, profoundly understand what is happening, and start taking action only when we are secure in our diagnosis. By slowing down we can see connections we couldn't before—we can ask better questions and arrive to more accurate conclusions.

An analysis in systems thinking often looks like this: we observe the data or occurrences related to the problem, trying to find patterns that repeat themselves over time. These patterns then can help us find the underlying structures of the problematic system. When we have a structure modeled out, it's easier to fine-tune interventions that create positive changes. Using these models, we can broaden our solution or intervention palette that may lead to better, longer solutions.

The main qualities of someone who is thinking in systems are curiosity, clear vision, openness to alternatives, courage, and compassionate understanding. People who want to be good at systems thinking need to be open-minded, and crave to understand the problem from every angle. This means that sometimes they need to abandon their opinion and embrace something that is contrary to their general thinking pattern. This kind of openness helps them embrace the stance of others, realize that problems are interconnected and never black-and-white, and accept that often there are multiple solutions to an issue.

Why should you learn to use systems thinking?

First, because this type of thinking allows you to find more solutions to a problem and a greater chance to find the best solution among them. You can expand the borders of your thinking, see problems in a new light, and articulate your diagnosis with more certainty.

Second, because while you will be able to identify more solutions, you'll realize that there is no solution without an impact on other areas of the problematic system. Every choice, every intervention we do is ultimately a trade-off. By being mindful about possible consequences, we can decrease the negative impact of the intervention. Using systems thinking can make better and more transparent decisions.

Third, the language and structure of systems thinking helps us present a problem better—we can tell a better story. Tools like loop diagrams and graphs can help you build a visual behind the story which further deepens understanding.

System thinking can be useful in solving many kinds of problems, but it helps a lot especially with the following:

16

- Important or urgent problems.
- Predictably reoccurring problems.
- Unpredictably reoccurring problems.
- Problems that couldn't be fixed before despite attempts.
- Problems that got fixed only on a symptom level.

Whenever you decide to take a closer look at a problem, refrain from blaming. It is tempting to point the finger to someone or something specific. "He is lazy, that's why the company struggles." or "She is a bully!" It is easy to cast blame on someone, but naming a scapegoat almost never fixes the issue.

What's the alternative? I will present it in a later chapter. But for now I'll only hint that approaching the problem from a position of curiosity, bringing it to the discussion table by asking exploratory questions, can go a much longer way.

Instead of making statements, ask questions such as:

- "Why is this problem a problem?"
- "Are there any aspects of this problem we don't understand?"

- "What are the most significant patterns in the problem?"
- "What outcome does the problem generate? What outcome would we like instead?"
- "How does the problem look on the following four levels: events, patterns, structure, and mental models?"

It's smart to keep your assumptions in your conscious awareness and tell yourself that whatever you assume, others may see the same picture differently. Others may operate with different assumptions and experiential background. It is important to map out and understand those perspectives to find a widely beneficial solution. Especially if we are talking about problems within an organization (workplace, classroom, company, social group, etc.). When we start investigating an issue, we need to bring everyone to the table, involve the different interest groups, and map out mental models together. This process can lead to solutions you'd never dream of.

A teaser of some of the most typical systems thinking tools:

a.) Causal Loop Diagrams

When it comes to causal loop diagrams, less is more. The goal of this diagram is to illustrate the problem in a simple way. You can add more items to the diagram as you progress in the story, but start by presenting the problem with the most necessary parts. A standard diagram may be sufficient to jumpstart the brainstorming session about alternative paths to look at the issue. If the issue is more complex, it's better to use multiple simple loop diagrams to illustrate the interrelationships between the elements of the system.

Contrary to what many people think about complexity, in causal loop diagrams it's acceptable to leave out elements and variables which don't make a change in the system and therefore are irrelevant to the analysis. Complex doesn't need to mean complicated.

The best causal loops show the connections and relations between the elements of the system and highlight the aspects that we are not conscious of. Loops are the simplified representations of the present. We'll learn about such loops later in this chapter.

b.) The Iceberg Model

When they were on their tragically ill-fated journey, the *Titanic* could have likely weathered the crash if it were not for the terrible damage caused to it by the massive portion of the iceberg that lay beneath the surface.

This is much the same case when people in a system are faced with a problem. At first glance, the concern and immediate focus may be on the tip of the iceberg that they can see: the event. Focus then immediately turns to figuring out what happened, with the concern being wanting to react to it quickly so that the fire (or ice) can be put out. But if you want to address more than the symptoms, and get to the root cause of the problem in order to prevent it from happening again, you can't spend all of your time near to, dealing with, and reacting to the event. You need to dig deeper, because that is where the real issues reside—and these shape the events as well as the trends (patterns of behavior over time, which allow us to forecast and predict what might come next).

The iceberg model distinguishes between the symptoms and the real problems exposing the underlying system structures. The structure is where you will find the policies, dynamics of power, perceptions, and purpose. If left unchanged, the structure is where the vast majority of damage to the system will come from, as the trends and events will continue to repeat themselves. The deeper your understanding of the system's structure, the more likely you will be to change the system's behavior in the long term.

Picture 1: The Iceberg Model[i]

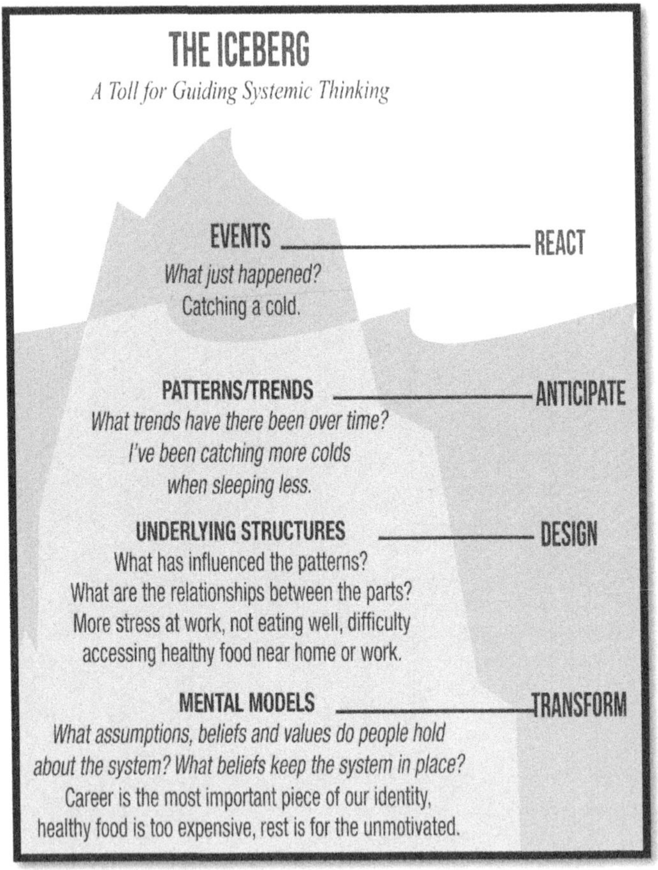

THE ICEBERG
A Toll for Guiding Systemic Thinking

EVENTS —————————— REACT
What just happened?
Catching a cold.

PATTERNS/TRENDS —————— ANTICIPATE
What trends have there been over time?
I've been catching more colds
when sleeping less.

UNDERLYING STRUCTURES ———— DESIGN
What has influenced the patterns?
What are the relationships between the parts?
More stress at work, not eating well, difficulty
accessing healthy food near home or work.

MENTAL MODELS ————— TRANSFORM
What assumptions, beliefs and values do people hold
about the system? What beliefs keep the system in place?
Career is the most important piece of our identity,
healthy food is too expensive, rest is for the unmotivated.

Let's talk about the levels of the iceberg you can see in Picture 1.

1. The Event Level

People perceive the world at the event level most of the time. For example, waking up in the middle of the night realizing that you're thirsty is an event-level analysis. Event-level problems can often be solved with a simple correction, like drinking a glass of water. However, the iceberg model encourages us to dig deeper instead of automatically assuming that the problem we are facing is indeed an event-level problem. Instead of just reacting to our thirst, let's dig deeper.

2. The Pattern Level

When we look beyond events, we often identify patterns. Events with strong resemblance have been occurring with us over time—we have been very thirsty during differing parts of the day. Maybe we are dangerously dehydrated. Acknowledging patterns helps us forecast and forestall events.

3. The Structure Level

When we try to find the answer to the question "What's the cause of the pattern we are observing?" we usually conclude that it's some kind of structure. Because of our increased workload in the heat of the day, we often forget to drink enough water, and this has taken its toll on our body in the summer heat. Professor John Gerber informs us that structures can include the following things:[ii]

- Physical things: stores, sidewalks, or benches in a park.
- Organizations: corporations, hospitals, and schools.
- Policies: regulations, restrictions, or taxes.
- Rituals: subconscious behaviors.

4. The Mental Model Level

The fourth level of the iceberg are the mental models, which are the collection of the attitudes, beliefs, expectations, morals, and values that provide structures continuous functioning. For example, the beliefs we subconsciously adopt and carry on from home or from our school, work, and surroundings. In the case of our dehydration, the mental model creating it could involve the belief that our job is more important than our health, that we need the money, or that by taking a short drinking break we might appear weak or lazy.[iii]

c.) The Archetypes

Systems archetypes are commonly repeating variations of feedback. Each archetype has a typical pattern of behavior over time, structure, and effective interventions. These archetypes help us to understand and quickly diagram the behavior of a system. The more you practice systems analysis, the easier you will notice and apply the structure when hearing an archetypical systems story.[iv]

Some systems can cause troublesome behavior through their structure. This trouble can take many forms. Some of the behaviors these archetypes create include addiction, low performance, and escalation. It isn't enough to just recognize the troublemaking structures and understand the problems they cause. They need to be changed.

People often make the mistake of trying to blame other people or events for the destruction these archetypes cause. In reality, the fault lies within the structure of the system.

So what can be done? We can escape these so-called system traps by being aware of their existence and using that knowledge to avoid getting caught in them. We can change the structure by revisiting our goals and developing new ones. We can work with the feedback loops to strengthen, weaken, or alter them—or even add new ones to the system.

The systems archetypes rapidly build systemic awareness and provide a simple and engaging way to communicate about systems to others. They are easy to understand. Working with classic stories helps people shift their thinking to a more systemic perspective. The classic stories are also an easy means of transferring learning about systemic issues from one situation to another.

If you successfully master the systems archetypes, you'll be familiar with the storylines and regular patterns of behavior over time. You'll detect them in real-world events and map their structure with ease. Also, by Going Deeper™ you'll be able to improve and enrich the structure of the specific system you'll be analyzing, adding implications for leveraged interventions.

The nine most common systems archetypes are the following:
- Shifting the Burden
- Fixes that Backfire
- Growth and Underinvestment
- Tragedy of the Commons
- Limits to Success

- Accidental Adversaries
- Escalation
- Drifting Goals
- Success to the Successful

When you tell a systems story with the help of an archetype, try to keep it simple if you're presenting it to people who are unfamiliar with systems thinking. In case your crowd is interested, you can tell them more about the archetype in question, but don't try to over-mystify the story with complicated terms people can't connect with. The best results come when people can find their own connection to the archetype in question. You can, however, facilitate understanding with simple yet widely known situations people can relate with. For example, when trying to explain escalation, you can refer to the arms race in the Cold War between the Soviet Union and the United States.

Test your knowledge.

Systems thinking is a skill that won't show itself in obvious ways. The more you practice the principles presented in my *The Systems Thinker* book series, the more emerged you become. Here are some tips to test your knowledge:

- The quality of your questions about approaching problems changed.

- Blaming and reductionist problem-solving slogans make you alert. For example, when you hear "The issue is that we lack [capital, knowledge, etc.]." you'll feel the need to ask questions that point beyond the simple problem diagnosis.

- You start to attribute certain problems to reinforcing or balancing feedback loops.

- You start mapping out mental models to think about an issue.

- You start to look for leverage points and bottleneck issues.

Many of these concepts may sound foreign to you, but don't worry, I will explain each of them in this book. The main focus of the current book is, however, mental models. If you wish to read more about systems archetypes, read my book *Learn to Think in Systems*.

Learning to use a systems thinking perspective together with its tools like causal loop diagrams, mental models (like the iceberg model), and archetypes will give you enough information to help you detect problems. To advance in your skills, study the archetypes, read the news, and approach stories from a systems thinking point of view. Tackle your workplace and personal life problems by looking at them as an outcome generated by the system you're in, and accept that there are limitations to fix certain issues.

Chapter 1: Essential Thinking Tools

Becoming a skilled systems thinker has a learning curve that includes the mastery of multiple cognitive skills.

How do we build up our systems thinking method?

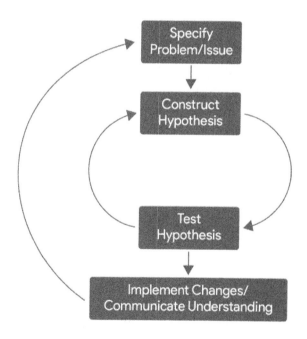

Picture 2: The Systems Thinking Method

First, we identify the problem we want to investigate. Then—preferably collectively within our organization or with the other people involved in the problem—we build a hypothesis to tell the story of the problem. After that, we need to test the hypothesis using different mental models. Finally, when we understand the problem and feel confident about our hypothesis, we can brainstorm possible changes.

When I talk about "models" here, I mean a structured plan that reflects a defined set of assumptions about how the world works. I need to highlight that all models are incomplete reflections of reality, therefore none of them are absolutely right. But some models are better than others. Models test our assumptions and theories. Ultimately, every model is only as good as the quality of the thinking that went into creating it.

So how can we improve the quality of our thinking? By learning additional, auxiliary thinking tools.

This sounds like an easy process in theory, but in practice we need to use a lot of thinking skills effectively to correctly articulate and test a hypothesis, create mental models, and implement the changes needed. Let's talk about these auxiliary thinking skills you can practice in isolation.

The Essential Thinking Tools

As you engage in systems thinking, you will see that some cognitive skills preponderate in each part. I collected the following thinking tools that systems thinkers want to practice:

- Creative and Analytical Thinking
- Systemic Thinking
- Synthetic Thinking
- Critical Thinking

Beyond these five, systems thinker and managing director and founder of High Performance Systems, Inc., Barry Richmond, formulated his list of thinking skills also invaluable to making better decisions:

- Dynamic Thinking
- System-as-Cause Thinking
- Forest Thinking
- Operational Thinking
- Closed-Loop Thinking

- Quantitative Thinking
- Scientific Thinking[v]

Creative and Analytical Thinking

Creative thinking is relating or producing a thing or idea that was not previously related. Creative thinking comes in handy when trying to solve problems when you're panicked. Some ideas might even be created to prevent panic. When I took my two children to Disney World, they were young enough to enjoy the amusement park, but not old enough to reliably remember their parents' names and phone numbers. I had temporary tattoos created for them with my name and phone number on them in case we got separated. Luckily, it never happened, but I got asked about where I'd gotten them from a lot of parents during our week-long vacation.

Creative thinking requires your imagination and can lead to a literal fount of ideas and solutions. Analytical thinking is convergent, meaning it pares down to a small number of distinct ideas, answers, or solutions for further analysis and utility. In comparison, creative thinking is divergent, meaning it begins with a description and then splits in many different directions to find many possible solutions. Convergent features include: logic, uniqueness, solutions, and being vertical. Divergent features include: imagination, multiple possibilities, solutions or ideas, and being lateral.

Using analytical thinking to approach a problem takes a deep and focused approach similar to tunnel vision to find all the necessary parts of the problem. Creative thinking is the opposite. It requires a wide-ranging approach of all possible options, including those that, on the surface, appear to be completely unrelated. I always think of creative thinking as opening the largest doors of your mind and letting everything flood in uninhibited. This is why it's thought of as lateral thinking, because the approach is wide.

Creative thinking has other benefits beyond problem-solving as well. It's actually good for you. The creative process can improve your health in a multitude of ways. One of those ways is that it's a stress reliever. There are many creative activities you can do to help relieve stress in your life, and you can tailor them to your own personal interests. Reducing your stress levels can help you prevent heart disease, Alzheimer's disease, and depression. Just have fun immersing in the creative process.

Creative thinking also increases and renews brain function. Creative tasks protect and encourage neuron growth by bolstering the growth of new neurons, which is vital in maintaining a healthy central nervous system. Creative activities can also help in recovering after a major illness or injury or stress such as a breakup or divorce. This can include crafting, brain games, and even listening to music.

Creative thinking also boosts your mood. No one on this Earth is 100% happy every minute of every day, and even happy people can experience periodic depression from time to time. Creative activities increase control over emotional pain and depression. It allows you a deeper understanding of yourself because you're connecting with yourself in a way that you normally couldn't or wouldn't.[vi]

Systemic Thinking

Systemic thinking is defined as an easy thinking technique for accessing a systematic understanding of complicated problems and situations. Systemic thinking allows us to manage any number of elements of a situation together rather than one at a time. It gives us the ability to use systemic focus in any situation.

It's important to note that systemic thinking, systems thinking, and systematic thinking are not the same thing. These are all different types of thinking, and they all have their own meaning. Systematic thinking is thinking in a methodical way whereas systems thinking is thinking about how things interact with one another. Systemic thinking is a simple technique used to identify a system-wide focus.

The basic idea behind systemic thinking is that everything interacts with the system around it, that everything affects and is affected by the person or system in its immediate surroundings. When approaching things from a systemic thinking mindset, we can no longer approach problems or situations as individual parts to be managed in isolation. We now have to take the parts together and manage them cohesively. We have to manage both the elements of the situation and how the parts interact with one another.

The systemic thinking process is a four-step process:

1. List as many system components as possible. This might include: problems, solutions, opportunities, needs, desired outcomes, and ideas.
2. Group common components together, and then state what each group has that makes them similar. From the above list, problems and needs might go together in the same group and desired outcomes, ideas, and opportunities could possibly go together in the same group.
3. Find a repeating theme across group descriptions.
4. Your process should look like: Components -> Subthemes -> Common Theme. This process really boosts your insight in any situation, and you might find yourself wondering why you haven't done this sooner.

It can be incredibly difficult to recognize patterns and themes when we first encounter a challenging situation. However, with practice and as our skills develop, we should be able to recognize them more easily or at least have the skill set to manage them more adeptly.

The experience of working with systemic thinking is more than just more knowledge and more skills.

It's more familiarity with the patterns and themes that will give you the ability to recognize them faster and easier. It is important to note that because the ability to recognize these themes and patterns can become ingrained in our brains over time, we may start to subconsciously recognize them without cognitively being aware of them.

This means we're not really comprehending what the pattern or theme means, we're just engaging in certain behaviors by rote because that's what we're used to. The idea is to purposefully find and understand the repeating patterns and themes in tough situations, as this allows us to continually improve and develop mastery and better insight in the realm of systemic thinking.

The process behind systemic thinking is to list as many components as you can possibly think of and then analyze and look for the similarities between the components.[vii]

Synthetic Thinking

When we break apart the different pieces involved in a situation it's incredibly easy to lose sight of how these parts interact with one another and within the situation, and this is how we end up in "analysis paralysis." This is because analysis tends to "shade" the interactions and make them more difficult to identify. When the interactions aren't as visible, our insight is also reduced, which can cause a situation to go from not so great to a mega disaster.

The tool we use to make sense of interactions and how things work together is synthesis. Synthesis is much more than simply putting something back together after you've taken it apart for an investigation. If analytical thinking helps us understand the different parts of a situation, then synthetic thinking allows us to truly understand how these parts work together. If analytical thinking allows you to dissect things down to their basic components, synthetic thinking allows you to find patterns across those components. Essentially, analytical thinking will help you pinpoint the differences while systemic thinking allows you to pinpoint the similarities.

Synthetic thinking is considered to be challenging because interactions can be harder to detect and manage. Synthetic thinking will help you find patterns and commonalities across a system or situation. What's more, while using this thinking tool you'll find these patterns, themes, and commonalities faster and easier.

As an example of synthetic thinking, let's look at the automobile industry, specifically advertising in the auto industry—an ongoing Dodge advertising campaign to sell trucks. For years, the company has identified trends in consumer information and consumer preferences to develop products and marketing strategies. These ad campaigns have synthesized several themes based on demographics, lifestyle characteristics, and psychographics. The ads promote strong and tough engines and bodies, the fact that Dodge is "made in America" and an American company, and even feature characteristics to appeal to families because the truck can morph into a "wagon" with some button pushing and seat rearranging. All of these parts are synthesized to persuade you to purchase a Dodge truck, no matter where you are in your life.

Critical Thinking

Critical thinking is the capacity to analyze facts, formulate and organize ideas, stand up for and defend opinions, compare and contrast items, draw conclusions, validate or invalidate arguments, and problem-solve. Critical thinking is based on assumption, an assumption that there is logic involved in problem-solving and it can be figured out and reasoned through.

Critical thinking is not going to be appropriate in every situation or when trying to make every decision. Take the example of romance. Critical thinking and logic cannot help you determine who to date or who to marry. These are decisions that will always be made by your intuition. This is also true for other items of personal taste. I will likely never be able to explain why I love Howard Chandler Christy's World War I recruitment posters for the United States. I'm sure it's because I also like his other artwork as well, and his ideal "Christy Girl." This isn't something I had to learn to love. It was automatic. But without a doubt there are important decisions in life that have to be thought about and mulled over, such as what college to attend, whether you should even attend college at all or if trade school is a better option, or if you should take that job on the other side of the country. Critical thinking is a metacognition otherwise known as thinking about thinking.

Critical thinking is important because it allows us to acknowledge our emotions but not be controlled by them, which is especially relevant when it's time to make a decision. Emotions are vital, especially to our memory and developing our personal tastes, but they can easily trick us too. They can mislead us into thinking we are making the right decision when we aren't. Have you ever heard that most eyewitnesses to crimes are unreliable? That's for many reasons. Sometimes it's due to outside influence, not getting as good a look at the perpetrator as the witness thought, or just the trauma of witnessing a violent crime. But it is well known amongst criminal trial attorneys and prosecutors that an eyewitness is one of the least reliable forms of evidence, and that is why circumstantial or forensic evidence to back up that witness testimony is always needed to help prove a person's guilt beyond a reasonable doubt. Luckily, critical thinking allows us to effectively handle our emotions by allowing us to sort through them and decide if they are appropriate for the current situation.

When a person uses critical thinking skills, the decision is made regardless of if the problem or situation is right or wrong. Once the critical thinker is provided with information, they analyze the information, interpret it, and then draw conclusions using what they also know about the world. All of this comes together, and the critical thinker forms their opinion on whatever topic is being investigated.

According to Dr. Roy van den Brink-Budgen, an expert in the field of critical thinking, there are four traits that are ingrained in critical thinkers: persistence, rigor, openness, and diligence. In addition, Dr. Robert Ennis, Professor Emeritus at the University of Illinois, has also developed a list of skills that successful critical thinkers should be able to perform.

- Judge the credibility of sources.
- Identify conclusions, reasons, and assumptions.
- Judge the quality of an argument— particularly its reasons, assumptions, and underlying evidence.
- Develop and defend a position on the issue.
- Ask the appropriate clarifying questions.
- Plan hypotheses or experiments, and assess experimental designs.
- Define terms in a way appropriate to the context.
- Be open-minded.
- Be well informed.

- Draw warranted conclusions, but with caution.[viii]

One of the key takeaways from this list is that all of these traits or skills are teachable. Every one of them can be taught or learned. Critical thinking isn't something you're born with, it's a skill you acquire with education and practice.

Dynamic Thinking[ix]

This thinking skill helps you articulate the problem in the frame of behavior patterns over time. Unlike static thinking where people focus on specific events, dynamic thinking focuses on events that unfold over time. It's not about a one-time event.

To improve this thinking skill, read and interpret behavior-over-time graphs like your annual sales report. If you have no access to such a graph from your own life, just research "behavior-over-time reports" on the internet and try to interpret them. Or listen to the evening news tonight, pick an interesting topic, choose a variable related to the topic, and look at that topic as just one blink of an eye in the over-time trajectory of the variable. For example, if you take the behavior over time of the stock market, you can look at events such as Black Monday as one—unfortunate and unpredictable—moment in the trajectory of stock market changes. When you think about how some events like Black Monday could be prevented or fixed, ask the following questions: "Over what period of time can this be reversed/stabilized? How much time does it take? What will happen to the main variables over time if we do X, Y, or Z?"

System-as-Cause Thinking

After you analyze a problem's behavior pattern over time, you want to build a model to present how and why the behavior is created and how can it be improved. System-as-cause thinking can help you choose what to include in your model and what to leave out. Making a system-as-cause analysis, you need to use only those elements and interconnections that fall in the direct circle of influence of the managers of the system: the people who manifest the behavior you wish to explain. This thinking model helps you identify those who hold the responsibility for the behavior in question.

Avoid operating from a blaming stance, though. Instead of leading a whodunit, encourage questions such as "How could we have been responsible?" Often, problems are not created by internal forces but external, yet we are still responsible for allowing the external force to influence us. Thus it's useful to ask, "What did we do to allow these external powers to control us?"

To develop system-as-cause thinking, try turning each "They did it." or "It's their fault." you encounter into a "How could we have been responsible?" It is always possible to see a situation as caused by "outside forces." But it is also always possible to ask, "What did we do to make ourselves vulnerable to those forces that we could not control?"

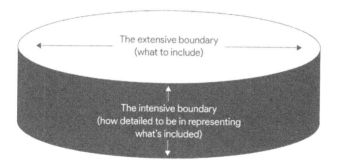

Picture 3: Extensive and Intensive Boundaries in the System

To build a good system-as-cause model, we can draw the extensive and intensive boundaries of the problem we are analyzing. As you can see in Picture 3, the extensive boundary is the latitude of what elements should be included in the model and the intensive boundary shows the depth of the elements included in the model.

Forest Thinking[x]

I bet you've heard the saying "You can't see the forest for the trees." This saying stays true in the so-called "forest thinking" as well. When we analyze the intensive boundaries of a problem, considering every single aspect—or tree—of it, we can lose our focus on what matters. Instead of trying to narrow down if a particular dishwasher stopped working on Sunday afternoon, it's more useful to see how often the dishwasher breaks down in general, how big the load is when it breaks down compared to the load when it works well, and so on.

Forest thinking shows us the "on average" state of a system. To improve your forest thinking skills, try to discover similarities rather than differences—especially when in an organizational setting. Just because every person has their own strengths, doesn't mean that they don't share some attributives—being useful for the company for instance. One person can be terrible at maintaining good relationships with the customers but can be exceptionally good at critical thinking. Instead of looking at individual factors, take a look at some central questions like "What is the interaction between the aspects guiding someone's work morale?"

Operational Thinking

Using operational thinking we try to understand how a behavior is created. The antithesis of operational thinking is factors thinking. We prefer to use the latter in everyday life, as we like to jot a lot of dots under a problem, list out which A, B, and C factors influence a problem. The shortcoming of this kind of thinking is that lists don't reflect the causality of these factors. Influencing and correlating with a problem doesn't necessarily mean causing the problem.

For example, if you think in factors thinking terms and you analyze what influences self-improvement, you could come up with a long list of factors (dissatisfaction with one's current life, major illness, getting fired, divorce, etc.). Using operational thinking, you might approach self-improvement as a process that coincides with external and internal changes. Operational thinking reflects the nature of the self-improvement process by unveiling its structure. Factors thinking only lists out the factors that can be connected to the choice of self-improvement.

To grow your operational thinking skills, ask questions such as "What is the nature of the process I'm looking at?" instead of "What is influencing the process?"

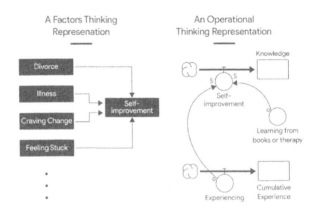

Picture 4: Factors Thinking vs. Operational Thinking.[xi]

Closed-Loop Thinking [xii]

Recall a scenario where you were discussing why your country performs poorly economically. When you enumerated the causes for the low performance, you probably mentioned governmental money mismanagement, bad leadership, and greedy banks as influencers of a low-performing economy. We call this kind of thinking linear or straight-line thinking. In this kind of thinking, A causes B, and causality works only one way. This is the cause—say, bad governmental money management—and this is the result—say, an underperforming economy. Also, linear thinking fails to capture the interrelationship between different causes and looks at them independently.

The "antidote" for linear thinking, Richmond says, is closed-loop thinking, which by any means is not closed-minded thinking. As you can see in Picture 5, closed-loop thinking captures the effect flow of the results which feed back to the causes. The causes are in a relationship with each other. Closed-loop thinking can help you see how causality is an ongoing stream of events and feedbacks and can't be captured accurately by a snapshot in time.

To improve your closed-loop thinking, try to observe the variables' shifting dominance over time instead of focusing on the most important variable.

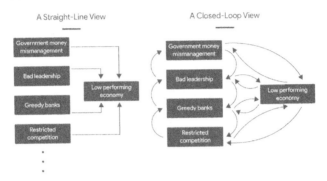

Picture 5: A Straight-Line vs. a Closed-Loop View of Causality[xiii]

Quantitative Thinking

In systems thinking, "quantitative" doesn't equal "measurable." Many elements of a system are hard or impossible to measure. We call them soft variables. These can be concepts like resilience, courage, motivation, and others. Some hard variables are also difficult to measure because of the nature of the system they exist within. For example, delays and information flow glitches can prevent accurate measurement of some hard variables.

While soft variables are inarguably important, they rarely are an aspect of analysis because of our inability to measure them. But they can be quantified. For example, in the case of an employee's confidence in decision-making, zero would mean that they have no confidence at all while one hundred would mean they are very confident in making decisions. While the numbers attached to soft variables are arbitrary, they are not ambiguous. If you want to strengthen the confidence level of your employees in making decisions in the following year, you can certainly quantify that. But you may not be able to measure it with exact numbers.

To advance in quantitative thinking, choose a soft variable that is not taken into consideration when trying to solve a problem—let's say in your workplace. Then think about how the problem would change or improve if this variable would be seriously considered in the problem-solving process. What could you or your company do to enhance the soft variable?

Scientific Thinking

First, let's talk about how science works. When we make a scientific analysis, we measure progress by getting rid of falsehood. Our truth of the moment is considered only a hypothesis until it's proven to be without any falsity. At the same time, many models are unscientific, yet their proponents talk about them as "The Truth." They sometimes rationalize these models' validity based on track record. Systems thinkers, like W. Edwards Deming, know that "all models are wrong, but some of them are useful."

Systems thinkers use scientific thinking to focus on simple numbers that are relevant to one another, instead of insisting on proving their models with exact numbers. They put their models under a lot of pressure testing. Systems thinkers want to know when and why their models fail.

Barry Richmond compared traditional thinking with systems thinking when he developed the thinking tools I mentioned before. Let's go through them one more time, comparing them directly:

1. Static thinking that focuses on specific events vs. dynamic thinking, which frames a problem based on the patterns of behavior over time.

2. System-as-effect thinking—which sees behavior created by a system as driven by external

forces—vs. system-as-cause thinking—which places responsibility for a behavior on internal actors who manage the structure of the system.

3. Tree-by-tree thinking—where one believes that true knowledge means distilling every detail—vs. forest thinking—where one believes that in order to know something, one should understand the context of relationships.

4. Factors thinking—where one thinks factors are the influencers or correlations with a certain result—vs. operational thinking—where one focuses on causality and understands how a behavior is created.

5. Linear thinking—where we see causality as a one-directional process where each influencing cause is independent from the other—vs. closed-loop thinking—where we view causality as an ongoing process.

6. Measurement thinking—where we're looking for the perfectly accurate and measurable data—vs. quantitative thinking—where you are comfortable with considering soft variables that can always be quantified but not always measured.

7. Truth-proving thinking—where one focuses on proving a model to be true—vs. scientific thinking—where one embraces that models always have a limited applicability.[xiv]

Chapter 2: What Are Mental Models?

To understand how to create mental models, first we need to understand what they are. The mental part is self-explanatory: something we conceive in our minds. A model is an abstraction or simplification of the real world. There are many types of models from matchbox cars, to how an earthquake is generated in natural history museums, to models simulating the activity of a black hole in space. Models bring the far away closer, the complex more approachable, for learning purposes. Let me repeat the systems thinking mantra, "All models are wrong, but some are useful." Their wrongness is in their simplicity, and their usefulness is in their potential to help us learn.

Okay, now what is a "mental model"? A mental model is a model that is created and tried in our conscious mind. "Conscious" in this sense implies awareness about our surroundings and our relation to the world.

Let's see a practical example.

Imagine yourself on the beach, gazing at the ocean. Your eyes capture light and focus it onto your retinas, which in exchange react by sending neural stimuli to the brain. As your brain receives the stimuli it creates the picture of the ocean in your mind. By this point, we've only addressed the visual information receptors. But this information doesn't tell you what an ocean is.

What makes you understand what the ocean is in your mind? At this point you start utilizing mental models. You start thinking about the ocean as something that exists in the world as a physical fact. The concept of the ocean is a model and it needs more information than your visual experience. It builds on your empirical knowledge. The ocean is salty water that is sometimes calm, sometimes waving and restless. It has high and low tides depending on the Earth's and Moon's position. It hosts a myriad of underwater animals and plants. I can claim these aspects of the ocean with confidence as they belong to the learned reality of my mental models. Based on this knowledge, I could build up new knowledge about the ocean if I chose to be a marine biologist.

In sum, mental models contain old empirical knowledge and have the potential to support new knowledge that is built upon the old.

Let's play a game. Take a look at the following three images and try to predict what will happen next. The images don't show what the next moment will bring but I'm sure you have an idea about it in your mind.

Pictures 6, 7, 8: What's Your Mental Model?[xv]

Your guess, in fact, is the simulation of a mental model you have about what's going on in the picture. You can come up with different outcomes than the obvious if you really try.

In the picture about sky diving, you could imagine the plane taking a sudden turn and the two people falling back on board.

In the second image, you could picture the dog missing the ball by a breath and awkwardly biting the air instead of nailing the catch.

In the last picture, you could simulate that the child pulls her hand back at the last second after

60

hearing the screams of her mother instead of pulling the pot on herself.

All this contemplation, of course, normally happens outside of our consciousness—we simulate our mental models as snap judgments.

How to use mental models in systems thinking?

As humans, we are generally comfortable and fluent at simulating mental models that fit our natural reality. But when things get more abstract is when hardship arises.

Jeremy Merritt, a systems thinker, uses the market system to give an example of an abstract system. Price in the market is the token of total demand for a product. The market can't be tied down to a physical place and you can't generate a concrete picture of it in your mind as you could with the ocean. Yet you accept that something invisible and untouchable such as the market exists and has an impact on your life.

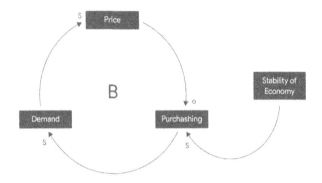

Picture 9: Price Deflation Loop

Let's take a closer look at what happened in the economic crisis of 2008. When the crisis became global and threatening, people started decreasing their spending and saving money instead. Retailers in turn started to struggle financially because of the huge drop in their sales, so they dropped their prices to try to incentivize consumers to spend more. Consumers were, however, aware of the price drop, and in the hopes that prices would further drop over time, they refrained from spending. We call this process price deflation and you can see it in Picture 9.

In the short run, customers acted in a rational way. In the long run, however, as the price deflation loop kept getting reinforced, and prices kept dropping, the income of companies also declined, which forced them to fire workers or go bankrupt. As more and more people got laid off, the national perception of welfare, security, and safety also declined. People feared spending, so they'd spend even less than before.

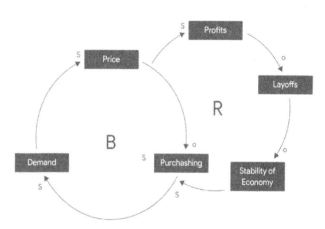

Picture 10: Economy Stability Loop

Economists needed to react quickly to the deflation by persuading policy makers to bring in some changes that would jump-start spending among consumers. In the US they used rebate programs like "Cash for Clunkers" or the first-time home buyer tax credit as tools to help the squeaky wheels of the economy get oiled again.

What should the boundaries (external and internal) of mental models be? When we talk about human mental models, they tend to have a narrow focus led by short-term incentives. But to simulate complex systems, we need to expand these boundaries. Even so, we're not great at mentally simulating multi-variable, interdependent systems with delays and multi-level feedbacks. We can, however, create computer programs to simulate complex systems with more reliability. We can build better mental models through software.

Complex Mental Models

Mental models are dynamic simulations of our reality. And in most cases they don't represent a challenge. There are other times, though, when we really need to sweat while playing out a simulation. Take a look at the chessboard in Picture 11. What's the status of the white player?

Picture 11: Chess Board Simulation

Did you catch that it's a checkmate? If you did, I bet it wasn't as easy as imagining the guys jumping out the plane to skydive. It takes much greater mental effort to map out possible future moves on a chessboard. Our working memory is limited, experts say, to seven items at the same time generally.[xvi] This means that we can't rely on only our brains when trying to simulate complex systems that often have more than seven variables, each interacting and feeding back to the others. Luckily, we have had computers at our disposal for the past few decades and we can level up our modeling to previously unimaginable heights. Literally. Things like space exploration, the internet, and advanced healthcare solutions are just a few benefits of computational modeling.

What makes a model useful?

We need models to aid and understand our decision-making. In order to make an informed decision, one has to have a clue about the system which one uses the model for. A medical-system–enhancing model, for instance, can only be as useful as how much you understand the system of medical organizations.

There are various computer simulation models; like an engineering design, a spreadsheet, dynamic models, etc. The utility of these models is largely determined by how well you can explain the results after modeling.

The model should be self-explanatory; otherwise, even if you get the results, all you can do is stare at a sheet with data you can't interpret. It is also a useful model if it provokes good questions. The answers to these questions might be embedded in the model. Through experimentation, you can arrive to helpful conclusions—and deepen your knowledge about the system in the meantime.

Testing and working with models—especially visual ones—provides a valuable feedback loop of learning.

Modeling dynamic systems.

If you think systems are hard to grasp, make them dynamic and you'll feel even more perplexed. Dynamic systems are composed of multiple mental models, not just one. Systems like the global economy, a country's healthcare system, or global aid projects can't be simplified into one single model. A series of mental models are needed to present how these systems function, what their bottleneck problems are, and what possible solutions there are to fix them. These systems have so many actors involved and they have so many interconnections that it's hard for our mind to simulate them.

Problems on the level of systems are non-linear. Non-linearity is a series of events in which one thing does not clearly or directly follow from another.[xvii] Systems also experience delays and reinforcing or balancing feedback mechanisms. The nature of systems dynamics is complex and hard to follow, and therefore you can often feel unsure about the proposed interventions to change them. What if something's missing? What if we didn't take something important into consideration?

Try to recall a recent complex problem presented in the news. Whenever a politician presents a proposal for change, it is followed by projections made by experts on what the consequence could be if the new law gets enforced—or if it isn't. Their assessment is usually vague, though, and provides little information about how the system's behavior will be affected due to the changes. The lack of information makes it difficult to grasp the system's dynamic and to have a real, meaningful debate on the subject.

There are some useful computer simulation software packages such as STELLA which can be helpful to provide a more holistic picture about the system.

What are stocks and flows?

Stocks

A stock is an agglomeration within the system. The classic example to illustrate a stock in systems thinking is a bathtub. Picture a bathtub which you can fill and drain.

The mental model of stocks and flows is a visual illustration of their cause-and-effect relationship. In STELLA, stocks are illustrated as a rectangle. Whatever that can accumulate, can be a stock. Can you think about anything?

Let me help: population. Money. Natural resources. Happiness. Energy.

Flows

The flow is the manager of the stock, so to say. It can add to the stock, take from the stock, or keep the stock in balance. If we go back to our example where the bathtub is the stock, then the rate at which the faucet delivers water into the tub is the flow. The stock in this sense is not the bathtub itself but the water that gathers in it. If you plug the tub and leave the faucet open, the water level increases and eventually overflows. If you unplug the bathtub and stop water from running, the stock of water will decrease. If you unplug the bathtub but leave the faucet running, the water level will increase, decrease, or stay the same depending on the speed of the inflow and the outflow.

Let's look at another example—like your bank account. The savings account increases in value as you put money in. If, let's say, you never spend and just save—so the money input stays at a constant rate—you'll experience a linear increase in your savings account over time.

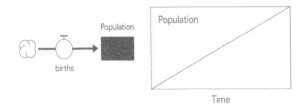

Picture 12: Savings Accumulation over Time

Similarly, your spending's flow on the model below removes money from your account, so the level of your fortune will drop over time. If, let's say, you never add money and just spend—so the money output stays at a constant rate—you'll experience a linear decrease.

Picture 13: Money Decreasing over Time

Bottlenecks

The first model we'll talk about is called the Theory of Constraints. This theory talks about how every system is limited by different constraints. One constraint, however, is going to be tighter than all of the other ones. The constraint that is the tightest of all is called the bottleneck. It's "the point of greatest congestion that is causing a delay within a system."[xviii]

The theory of constraints implies that the system's performance is going to be limited by the bottleneck. If there is no change to the bottleneck, the system will not improve. When the bottleneck is influenced, the system changes.

We can think about the theory of constraints in the context of our own lives. Many of us don't know what our bottlenecks are. If we fail to address this key issue, we'll fail to move forward in life or see anything change. We don't need to work harder on our self-development; we just need to identify where to concentrate our efforts.

You struggle in your relationship. You lash out at your partner often without knowing why and you feel insecure, which exacerbates your number of outbursts. You read books on anger management, practice meditation—you pay for a Tony Robbins seven-day seminar using all your savings. You do everything humanly possible to become a more patient and kind person, but after a month of chill and post-Tony Zen, you lash out again. Why?

Because all the humming on the mountaintop, all the mumbo jumbo, and all the optimal personality growth were just symptoms of your main issue: your early relationship with your dad.

Once you can stand in front of him, look him in the eye, and say "I understand that I ended up with this mentality because you told me this is the right way. You were never really there for me except when dispensing a few encouraging words, but leaving me alone in the matter nevertheless... I learned through the years when I couldn't rely on you to believe that one can't rely on men. That they often lie, as you did. I know that you gave me the best you could according to your best knowledge. It will be a long journey to change, but I'm up to it. I forgive you." the bottleneck won't disappear. Your dad won't change, probably, and your upbringing won't be erased, but now you'll be able to move on and truly change. Now you'll know that you're not a crazy person.

Every system error has a bottleneck—economic, political, and/or social issues. There is one problem which, if treated, can make it easier for the system to change and improve. It is not a guarantee that anything will change in the end.

But it is a guarantee that as long as the bottleneck issue is not addressed, nothing will change.

Leverage

Leverage influences a system to "return the maximum effect per a unit of effort." Today, our attention is scattered and our time and energy is limited compared to how many options we have. However, we can maximize the benefits of our time and energy by using leverage.

What do I mean by that? If we consider that time, energy, and focus are interchangeable, we can "exchange" them to get the most benefit. For example, sometimes you can use more of your energy and focus to win time. Let's say you need to leave work two hours early to attend your kid's graduation. You can invest more energy and focus to finish your daily tasks at work to "win" enough time.

The Pareto Principle, or the 80/20 rule, talks about how 80% of one's results can be achieved with 20% of one's effort. Most of us already know that, but that's not what's truly important in the image you can see below. Instead, if you move down the line, you'll see that "50% of one's results can be achieved with just 1% of one's effort."[xix]

You should want to be on the straight line. Some tasks don't require all our expertise, and the marginal return any extra investment of time, energy, or focus brings is simply not worth it.

My friend and role model, Derek Sivers, told me a story once. He used to bike down Venice Beach every morning when he lived in LA. He was kind of competitive about it. He was biking as hard as he could, huffing and puffing, investing all his might and energy into the process.

He went up and down the beach in 43 minutes.

He didn't enjoy it. Every day, it was more and more burdensome for him to go out and bike because he knew the physical pain he'd feel. So one day, he changed his mind. He didn't rush; he casually biked, enjoying the view. When he was done, he surprisingly experienced that he'd ridden the same distance in 47 minutes. All that suffering and huffing and puffing was for an extra four minutes.

Many of us spend too much effort and don't get the desired results, or we feel like the outcome was not worth the effort, as Derek did. You have to learn what level of expertise is needed to hit your goals. Donella Meadows has three things that are considered to be the most important leverage in a system.

The first is changing the rules. This can help define what is possible within the system. What rules can you change in your system called life? Your habits, what you invest energy and time in, which areas of your life you focus on… these can all optimize your efficiency.

The second is building in self-organization. This means designing your system in a way that it will improve naturally over time. These can be self-made constraints and checkpoints—for example, setting your alarm clock for two p.m. each day to ask yourself, "Am I productive?" It can also be deliberately not buying sugar or chocolate when you are on a diet, packing away your videogames into the attic, and so on.

Finally, the third important leverage is improving the information flow. We can reflect more accurately on our progress if we introduce objective and accurate measuring tools like feedback loops. They are loops because they are inspecting information as a circulation, and not in a linear nature. The feedback itself is a tool of information delivery—it informs how a system is doing relative to the goal of the system. For example, if you are constantly arguing with your partner about nonsense, you might be in a reinforcing negative cycle. You need to be aware of this negative loop you are in to be able to talk about it and break out of it.

What you'll want to do is minimize delays between measurement and improvement. Imagine yourself as a product that needs improvement. It should be fast and consistent. A daily testing, measuring, and installing of improvements on your system can create better leverage. If you work on a daily basis to improve your relationship, for example, it will normalize quicker.

Feedback Loops

Feedback loops are the engines of the system— they keep the system running. While mentally it is hard to imagine them, by having a computer simulation they can become quite transparent.

Take a look at Picture 14. The line leaving the bubble of money input rate and pointing at money input shows a dependent relationship between the two elements of the system. In the model in Picture 14, the money flow is dependent on the money input rate and also savings level, as the level of interest depends on the total amount of savings. The more money you have, the more interest you earn that feeds back to the money inflow.

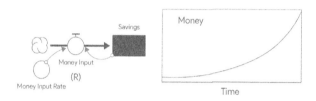

Picture 14: Money Growth over Time

The money input rate is illustrated using a converter. Converters can include constants that you can utilize to alter other elements of the model. The money input flow is determined as savings × money input rate. By illustrating the money input rate with a converter, we can see more clearly that the flow of money input is a function of both savings and money input rate.

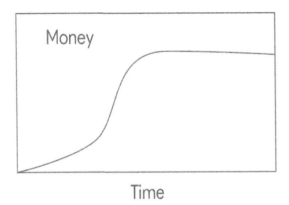

Time

Picture 15: The Function of Savings and Money Input Rate

The structure thus generates a reinforcing feedback loop. Can you see the savings stock showing an exponential growth over time? In this model there is no limit to growth. It would be great if this were a realistic model, but in real life we also have expenses which will limit the growth of our piggy bank. This can be illustrated by a balancing loop.

The relationship between the size of your savings and the expense rate form a balancing loop. The expense rate shifts based on the size of the savings account and therefore limits the growth of your savings. If you spend more, your savings account depletes. The less money you have in your account the less interest you earn, so the growth of your account slows down and grows at a slower rate—or worse, it slowly starts decreasing.

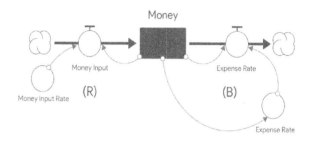

Picture16: Money Inflow and Outflow

With this simple example, we laid down the groundwork of a system's main building blocks—namely stocks, flows, converters, and connectors—and how they are interconnected by feedback mechanisms. Now you can build and explore real models of complex systems.

So how do we use the knowledge we've gained about bottlenecks, leverage, and feedback loops? When we identify a bottleneck, we should devote our time to using the highest leverage until the bottleneck is no longer a problem. Then we measure our improvement-detecting feedback loops. Then we move on to clear our next bottleneck. The more bottlenecks we overcome, the less constraining the next bottleneck will be. This is a cycle where each repetition will push us to a higher level of emergence. "Shortly: find your bottleneck, experiment to remove it, repeat."[xx]

A classic illustration of systems dynamics.

Let's dig deeper into the world of complex feedback systems using an example from nature: predator-prey dynamics. When we analyze the dynamics of a single population, we normally consider the natural growth rate and carrying capacity of the species in the environment. But in the real world, no species lives in isolation. They interact with other species, thus affecting each other's rate of growth or decay. Here we'll take a look at two specific species. The example comes from Duke University, presenting a set of data from the Hudson Bay Company in Canada of lynx and snowshoe hare pelt trading records.[xxi]

The model starts showing data from 1845, an impressive length of time. The records can help us deduce the population levels of both species. I must add that there are some simplifications to this model. We need to make the following rather steep and unrealistic assumptions:

- The specific predator depends singularly on the specific prey as its food supply.
- The specific prey's capacity as food supply is infinite.
- The specific prey has no other natural enemies, just this specific predator.

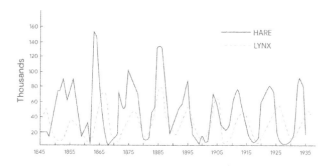

Picture 17: The Dynamic between the Lynx and Snowshoe Hare Population

While there are very few cases where a specific predator is the singular consumer of a specific prey, the Canadian lynx and snowshoe hare are pretty close to this condition. (Human involvement such as trapping these creatures for fur and other reasons significantly impacted both species, but let's not take this into consideration to keep the model simple.)

Take a look at Picture 17. What do you think about its oscillation pattern? Quite drastic and interesting, right? What kind of dynamic between the lynx and hare is responsible to create this oscillation?

Before we move on to answer this question, I'd like to add that in some regions of Canada, the lynx died out. The snowshoe hare population, however, didn't stop oscillating. This information hints the existence of another predator for the snowshoe hare. But let's not complicate our model with this information either for now. I just mentioned it so I can illustrate to you how complex and interconnected even simple systems such as this one can be.

Understanding the predator-prey system dynamic.

While many external factors influence the birth and death rate of the hare-lynx population dynamic—such as habitat destruction, urbanization, and weather changes—the most drastic changes can be shown through birth and death rates. So let's build a model around that.

Let's use the same model structure we used for your savings account.

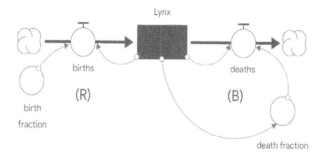

Picture 18: The Birth and Death Rate of Lynx

Just as it stood true in the case of money, the more lynx you have in the stock, the more lynx will be born. The feedback mechanism at work is a reinforcing one. (See structure R in Picture 18.) However, if we have more lynx preying on the same amount of hares, they will also die at a faster rate due to insufficient food resources, so the population growth gets balanced. (See structure B in Picture 18.)

The population growth of the lynx will show an S-shaped growth—there will be a quick growth over time, the number of lynx will peak at some point, then it will stop and stabilize at a level at which the lynx population is sustainable in the system. The population grows or decreases following the simple rule of thumb of having enough resources to sustain it.

As you can imagine, the story is more complicated than this. So far we have a competing balancing and reinforcing feedback loop. The reinforcing loop is dominating the system at first, thus the grown in the population. But then we can experience a shifting dominance as the balancing loop diminishes the growth. The birth rate and death rate of lynxes are in balance at this point.

Before I go on with the story, stop for a second and try to guess what kind of feedback mechanism is responsible for the oscillation between the hare and lynx populations.

Did you take the time to think? Okay, let's go on.

Let's collect what we know for sure. First, I could have used the same graph and mental model in the case of the hare population as well. Their population grows until they hit the carrying capacity of the ecosystem they live in. The hare and lynx populations are not isolated, however—

they depend on each other. Let's model this dependence.

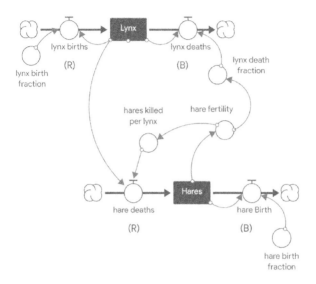

Picture 19: Dependence between the Lynx and Hare Population

In Picture 19, you can see that the stock of lynx is connected with the deaths of hares. Also, the stock of hares is connected with the deaths of lynx through an added variable: hare density. Why? Because the survival of a larger portion of lynx depends on the amount of hares in the region.

Now that we have a model, let's experiment with different scenarios.

Experimenting

Let's start with the premise that the population levels of hares and lynx are in dynamic equilibrium. In other words, the death and birth number of both species are the same. We start our experiment like this because it is easier to spot changes that diverge from a state of equilibrium.

Let's make the model more realistic and introduce a new variable into the picture: hunting for fur.

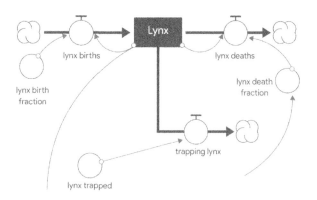

Picture 20: The Effect of Hunting on the Lynx Population

The stock of lynx has an additional element now, the outflow due to trapping. To keep the dynamic equilibrium on the model, let's assume trapping starts only 10 years after we started our analysis. With the help of the computer simulation from STELLA, the scenario would look like this, as 100 lynx get trapped and removed from the stock of lynx and the trend continues over time. (Lynx are represented by the line on the bottom.)

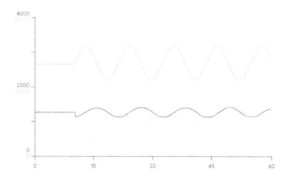

Picture 21: Simulation with 100 Lynx Trapped over Time

Let's mix things up a little and say 500 lynx get trapped. Then the simulation would look like this:

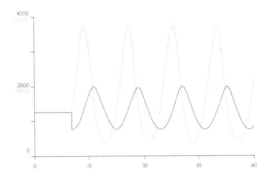

Picture 22: Simulation with 500 Lynx Trapped over Time

The oscillation begins on a smaller or larger scale once the population of lynx drops due to trapping. How does this change affect the hare population? We discussed that in this model the population of hares depends only on the population of lynx. What happens, then, if the number of the furry predators suddenly decreases? As there are not so many predators around, the hare population doesn't get hunted in the regular way. They are less hunted, thus the number of the hare population suddenly increases. (See the oscillation.)

How does the increase of the hare population affect the lynx population in return? Well, there is more food for every lynx now, so the lynx population also starts to grow with a slight delay. The reinforcing loop of births becomes dominant again.

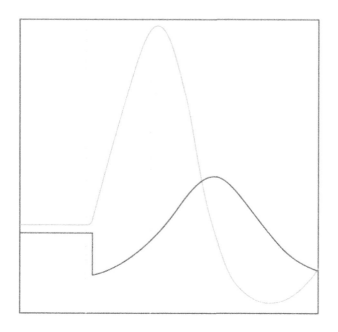

Picture 23: Snapshot from the Oscillation Graph

Let's take a closer look at what's happening: the straight line of the lynx population slowly reaches the same level as it was before the trapping, meanwhile the hare population outstandingly peaks. By this point there are enough lynx around to limit the growth of the hare population. (See

Picture 24.) In other words, lynx are consuming hares faster than hares can reproduce. There is a shifting dominance occurring, where the balancing loop of the hare population limits the growth of the species.

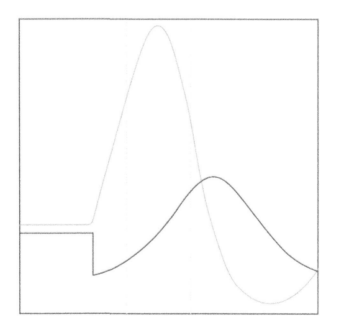

Picture 24: Second Close-up

Following the peaking of the hare population growth, the lynx population steadily continues to grow. For the next few years the population of hares decreases and the population of lynx increases. The dominance shifts to the reinforcing loop of the lynx population. In this scenario, there are still plenty of hares left to feed the lynx population. See Picture 25.

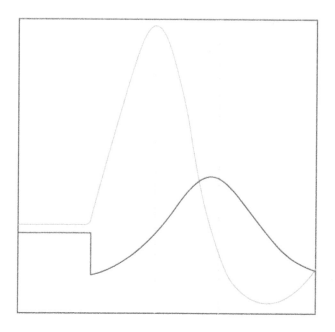

Picture 25: The Dominance of the Reinforcing Loop of the Lynx Population

However, over time, the lynx population growth slows down as the population of hares decreases to the level where another shift in dominance happens and the balancing loop of the lynx population becomes the most significant. In other words, there are not sufficient hares to sustain so

91

many lynx. This causes a sudden death rate increase in the lynx population—they die of hunger. This process generates the same dynamic as trapping lynx did. It jumpstarts another loop of hare population growth which, over time, will collapse again. And the oscillation happens again and again.

Let's recapitulate what we just did here. We unearthed the cause of the oscillation with the help of the feedback mechanisms at work affecting the two populations. Thanks to this we got a more profound understanding about the two-species system and its two interdependent balancing loops. This new clarity, of course, answers some of our questions, but also creates new questions such as:

> - What would happen if people started hunting hares instead of lynx? Would the system show the same behavior?
> - Can we stop the oscillation? How?[xxii]

The Lotka and Volterra equation.

Lotka and Volterra were both mathematicians in the first half of the 1900s. They are the fathers of a couple of nonlinear, differential equations meant to illustrate the predator-prey system dynamics. Oscillations such as the ones we observed in the predator-prey system can be found in the system of economy. The equations created by Lotka and Volterra thus had a big impact on the development of economic theory. Being able to understand the causes of such oscillations helps us identify the structures that are responsible for this behavior. And also, we're able to design better solutions for dampening the oscillations and stabilizing crucial systems such as the economy.

Chapter 3: Causal Loop Diagrams

Causal loop diagrams are mental models that serve us to present cause-and-effect relationships within the system. There are, however, some less understood, unspoken processes behind these connections.

How does a change in a company's reward system affect a worker's performance? How does a change in the amount of funds available for research and development affect the discovery of new technologies?

Taking a deeper look at the links presented in such cases can help us become more cognizant of the structures that create the observed behavior. We then can find more fitting solutions to fix the behavior. Going Deeper™ is a process in systems thinking where we add thought bubbles to causal loop diagrams and thus explore the not-so-obvious parts of a system.

When you go deeper, you create a causal loop diagram on which you illustrate the problem in the system. The second step is to look for connections that are created by human choice (versus hard physical structures). For example, if you have a connection where a change in weather conditions affected the crops, we're facing a problem created by nature. But if we analyze a connection between a change in governmental funding and investment in cancer research, that's a case that includes human choice.

After you pin down a few connections that are considered human choice, you can start digging deeper, asking questions like "Why was this choice made?" To physically illustrate the process of thinking, we attach a thought bubble to the connection, which will represent the implicit thought processes going on around the topic.

"What do we put in the thought bubble?" you may ask. Ideally, you (or your group) try to position yourself in the situation. You can use think tank methods, role plays, try to empathize—whatever works. The thought bubble should include the rational thinking path of each of the elements acting in the loop.

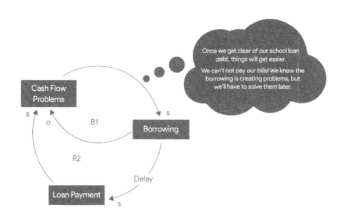

Picture 26: The Causal Loop of Borrowing

Let's say you and your family are facing some financial difficulty, so you need to borrow some money from your bank. (See loop B1 in Picture 26.) However, this is not your only loan and the accumulation of debt and interest payment pushed you into an even worse financial crisis. There's no way out, you need to borrow again. (See loop R2 in Picture 26.)

How to design the causal loop.

There is a directly proportional process going on in this example. As the cash shortage problem increases, so does the borrowing problem. Then an inversely proportional event happens—as money thanks to borrowing increases, the cash shortage problem decreases. This is what you see in loop B1. But as times goes on, loan payments rise and cash shortage becomes a burning issue again, as you can see in loop R2. This situation is a classic systems archetype story, namely Fixes That Backfire.

As I said before, the thought bubble has to be added to the connection that represents human choice. In our case, the human choice is fixing the money shortage problem by borrowing. Thus we added the bubble to the line connecting "cash flow problems" and "borrowing." Assuming that we are acting rationally when we decide to borrow, we should ask ourselves what rational reasons we have to undertake an extra loan. Maybe we just want to stay afloat for now, hoping for a better future—a promotion, a heritage, paying off the debt with the highest interest rate, etc. We could also be acting out of desperation—we are hungry now! We know another loan won't solve our long-term problems, but the short-term issues are much more life threatening. There could be some emotional aspect at play such as not wanting your children to notice something is wrong or to worry.

Focus on multiple perspectives when you fill the thought bubble. Perhaps you're looking forward to that long-promised promotion. Your wife maybe is looking forward to go back to work after a hard illness. Capturing multiple positions helps you have a more accurate grasp on the situation.

The point of Going Deeper™ is to detect and pinpoint those not-so-obvious reasons for a behavior that are not on the surface. Jumping to premature judgments like "We're so irresponsible." or "We don't have any financial education." will provide premature solutions that will not help the situation. It's always better to go and learn about every individual problem a few layers deeper than the obvious.

Menu Development

Let's look at another example.

The chef of a famous restaurant gets appointed to create and release a brand new vegan menu for the newest restaurant in a chain with specific ingredients, fitting today's increased demands for vegan food with the restaurant's top-notch quality standards. The plan was to experiment and finalize it within a short time frame, using a small crew of cooks, dieticians, and tasters.

In month one, when they begin the project, the release of the menu is scheduled for month four, but then it has to be delayed until month seven as a few recipes seem to not hit the restaurant's standards. In month seven, the grand opening is delayed again in order to add even more dishes. In month ten, the release is again rescheduled a full year after the original opening plans.

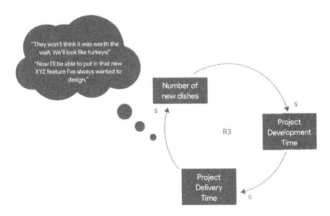

Picture 27: Menu Delivery Delay

To capture the mental model of this story, let's draw a causal loop diagram. Its elements are the number of recipes, the projected development time, and the projected delivery date. It looks like the more the delivery date gets pushed back, the more recipes the chef wants to add to the menu. Why is this happening?

Let's dig deeper into the cognitive process of the clearly human-made decision of creating more recipes as the release date gets delayed. Thus we put the thought bubble on the line between number of recipes and projected delivery date.

One likely reason is that the restaurant owner thinks he needs to compensate with something for the delay. "If my menu is not amazing, the customers will think the wait was in vain."

From the chef's perspective, the delay could be an opportunity to experiment with new dishes. "Luckily I have some extra time to try out the recipe I always wanted."

By thinking deeply enough about the hidden reasons of the actors that create a problem in the system, we can discover additional variables that we can paste into our mental model. We could assume that the longer the delay, the more people can taste-test the sample menu; the chef can make a more informed decision about what people like and dislike in general; the more opportunities to improve those recipes that surely will go on the menu; to optimize the kitchen storage based on demand; and so on. Going deeper and deeper into the motivations of the actors in the system may reveal interconnections we didn't think about upon our initial assessment of the issue.

Before trying to fix complex problems, we want to gain a deep understanding about the underlying thought processes that go into a decision. Thanks to this understanding we will be able to design more effective actions. Rigorously examining our mental models can lead us to deeper insights and better actions that we wouldn't have known unless we did the digging first.[xxiii]

Make your own mental model.[xxiv]

Making a mental model is like telling a story—if you get a good story, you'll gain a deeper understanding about the characters' motivations, reality, and mindset. If we tell our story well, it can help us make sense of our own life better. In the following paragraphs I'll take you through the creation of causal loops as mental models.

1. Choose the problem.

To get started with your mental model, you need to find an explicit problem in a system that you want to investigate. Then comes the phase of data collection. It's always more interesting to examine problems long existent or persistent despite our best efforts to fix them.

For example, in one hospital, senior ER doctors had charged a group of residents with improving their knowledge in wilderness medicine by forming a wilderness medicine research team. This meant going through documents, previous data on patient handling, problematic areas, and trying to come up with faster and better interventions.

In principle, the residents understood the long-term benefits of investing energy and time in this field of emergency medicine, but the many daily demands on their time often kept them more focused on their regular ER duties.

Over time, the team grew comfortable with not preparing for their presentations or in investing little time in superficial research, and attendance at wilderness medicine research meetings began to decline.

2. Force-Field Analysis

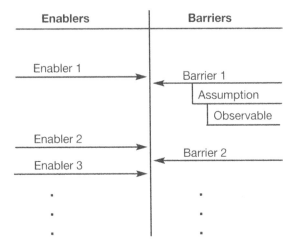

Picture 28: Force-Field Analysis Template[xxv]

Step two in creating explicit mental models is to do an interview session with the people who are involved with the problem. In this process you want to pick the brains of these people and try to make sense of their motivation and thinking patterns. Ask them to:

- Share the chronology of important events.
- Clarify their part in the situation/problem.
- Create a modified force-field analysis of the situation.

Managing a deep force-field analysis requires:

- Tracking down barriers and enablers to reaching the objective.
- Making clear the assumptions behind these barriers and enablers.
- Giving clear examples that illustrate each one. (See Picture 28.)

3. Select important variables and "scrub."

Once you have the initial story of the problem, it's time to find the most important variables. These can be either the most often mentioned variables or those that are explicitly mentioned to affect key performance measures.

In the hospital example, important variables might be "senior doctor's expectations," "wilderness medicine improvement's importance," or "regular ER duty overload."

When analyzing the data gathered from the interviews, be vigilant for expressions of subjective experience of variables such as "too much work," "lack of time or energy," "bad management," or "having no life." Then peel off the layer of subjectivity by scrubbing the expressions of qualifying adjectives. Make sure to make the data judgment or conclusion free.

4. Describe variable relationships.

Step four requires you to find other variables that are closely connected to every significant variable. The more interconnections you identify, the better. Look for causes, consequences, and constraints that connect these variables.

For example, in the story with hospital residents, we can connect "too much work" with the "lack of time and energy" variable with an S line, which means they change in the same direction—the more ER workload the residents have, the more they will lack the time and energy to do their research work.

These variable pairs will be the cornerstones of our causal loop diagram.

5. Tell the story.

We need to find several variable pairs to find a common story running through them all. The common story will guide us in developing such a model that includes only those aspects that are relevant in the problem. The story should be systemic and have clear feedback mechanisms, which means the events should also be recurring.

The title of the hospital story could be "Improvement without Time and Energy," to portray the dynamics of the resident team. The research effort failed due to a lack of time and energy for those who were responsible for it. From the residents' perspective, the researching task was secondary to their more urgent daily demands.

6. Build a causal loop.

Once upon a time, a causal loop designer had to start connecting the relevant variables in the shape of a loop to create a causal loop diagram. The storyteller had to be vigilant to ask questions like "Why did this occur?" and "What did this affect?" to identify more undiscovered causal connections.

In other words, create the loop diagram by adding all the variables and linking them with S (same direction) or O (opposite direction) connections. Add variables until the full story is told. Pay attention to delays where relevant.

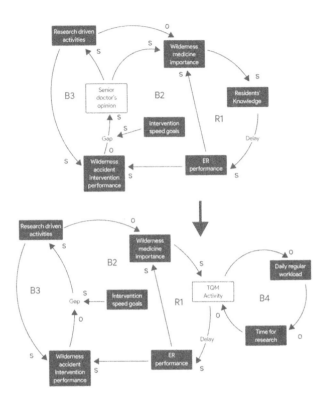

Picture 29: The Current Working System at the Hospital

The first causal loop diagram (top) describes the belief by senior doctors that research and development of the importance of wilderness medicine would increase wilderness accident-related intervention quality (R1).

However, they were also focused on research-driven activities that would reduce a gap between wilderness accident intervention performance and overall ER performance (B2 and B3).

In the bottom diagram, loop B4 is added to capture the dynamics of regular work demands that take time away from research activities.

In the ER hospital example, senior doctors believed that as awareness and skillfulness of wilderness accident intervention increased, the quality of problem handling by general ER doctors would increase. This would eventually lead to improved long-term medical performance, which should further increase the importance of research and development in specific ER fields (loop R1). But senior doctors also wanted to make sure general ER duties were done. And as research-driven activities increased, it would have taken time away from regular ER activities.

The link to the variable "Work Backlog" is very important, as it illustrates the pressure and overwhelm that accumulates when the ER gets very busy. This balancing loop captures the dynamics of residents being regularly interrupted either by an emergency case in the ER when they want to do research or by the stress of not being able to finish their research when they do their regular ER tasks (B4).

7. Finalize the causal loop diagram.

When you're done sketching your diagram, double-check it to make sure it illustrates the story correctly. Track down logical fallacies if there are any. Make sure that all the cause-and-effect relationships are well presented. Then make sure the variables tell the story at the same level.

I purposefully added "Senior Management Attention" to the loop to make this point now: it's an unnecessary variable, as it's not relevant. After the task was dispensed, they were not taking an active role in the story.

If you make any meaningful changes after the revision of loop details, go through the entire story once more and make sure the information gathered from the interviews are still well represented.

When designing causal loop representations of mental models, we focus on the accurate illustration of an individual's beliefs instead of capturing the world as it is. Mental mapping helps us gain new insights by organizing experiences and motivations in a relational framework.

110

Chapter 4: Shared Mental Models

In Star Wars, the popular sci-fi series, Jedi can communicate and share their thoughts with each other without actually talking. Unfortunately, we regular mortals don't have this skill. More so, we often struggle to deliver our thoughts to others in a clear way—we make assumptions and often misunderstand each other. The basis of our communication lies in our mental models, the interpretations of reality we have in our head about the world. Based on these models, or mental maps, if you like, we interpret, judge, and make choices. In other words, our mental models control our actions.

Even though our mental models play such a vital role in our lives, we are often unaware of the specific connections and interpretations within them. Not many people are self-reflective at that level; not many of us test our own thinking, compare our actions and their outcomes to our desired actions and outcomes.

Things get even more complicated when we want to think in a group. Trying to find a shared understanding can be difficult when we don't really understand our individual thinking process either. We, as humans, are wired to look for answers within our own knowledge and memory framework. When facing an opinion that is opposing our own, our gut response is to defend our position, not to test our mental models with the new information and then see if it still makes as much sense as we think. We often operate on autopilot and don't examine our assumptions and beliefs critically. These statements are true in the case of most people. So imagine the chaos that can happen if ten of such people try to think together.

When thinking in teams, the window of possible opinions and interpretations has to be widened. We need to build a continuum of possible positions instead of a narrow right-or-wrong stance. By allowing a broad spectrum of positions when thinking about complex issues, we will increase the chances of deeper involvement and better communication.

Apart of individual thinking, people working in an organization form mental models about the relationships and interactions within the group as well—this is what we call group thinking. Such thinking involves the shared opinion about organizational values, norms, power distribution, status, core beliefs, company direction, basic rules, and so on.

However, underlying problems and opinions are often not shared in group thinking. Yet, they can surface accidentally. Such subtleties involve levels of satisfaction at the workplace, hidden rivalries, contempt towards coworkers or managers, lost motivation, etc. Bumping into people's hidden soft spots can make them defensive; they can lose motivation even further.

Management teams have to keep their subordinates in check but also make them feel heard, cared about, and important. This scenario flows through many levels of the organization's hierarchy. Board members need to keep the shareholders happy. They need to keep their direct employees like department managers happy. These managers need to keep their subordinates content, and so on. In this process of team building, due to familiarity, members start forming opinions of other members (she is reliable; he's always late; she gets lost in the details; he takes rushed decisions, and so on). Yet, the mental models of these people are not so obvious and they rarely get explored.

To manage an organization effectively, members need to know how other members think, not only how they behave. Shared mental models help this endeavor. Having a shared mental model and knowing how the members of an organization think can enrich the organization with new talents, thinking skills, and alternative solution strategies. People also get better at accepting diversity and being self-reflective. Let me share an example of a group-thinking approach.

A company going green.[xxvi]

A public utility firm's senior leaders decided to reach out to board members and engage them in a project of change, namely, making the company more green. Like everything else in this world, change has a price. The board members should be down for investing into these changes. Systems thinking expert Charlotte Roberts partnered with the leader of the environmental science department to find an acceptable way of presenting the continuum of positions the board could embrace.

Choosing between Environmental Stewardship and Environmental Leadership engaged the executives and directors a lot, and a deep dialogue took place over these positions. Environmental Stewardship would incorporate activities inside the organization. They would keep a sharp eye on evidence that proves the green initiative would be a sound decision from a financial point of view, providing acceptable return on investment. Thus Stewardship is a more risk-cognizant approach. Environmental Leadership would put a great emphasis on research and development, experimentation, introduction of new technologies, and teaching people about new discoveries. This is a more costly and financially risky approach.

The left end of the continuum, Compliance with Regulations and Follower of Best Practices, are the conventional standards based on which companies operate. They are relatively risk free.

Picture 30: Continuum of Choices

When we're presenting a continuum of positions like the one above, it isn't necessary for the entire organization to sign up under one position. They can comply with regulations in some areas, in others follow best practices, and in some commit to innovation to benefit a higher cause like environmental protection. Leaders on the board admitted that they'd like to embrace what Environmental Leadership entailed but they had shortage of budget for the moment. Even though the company couldn't fully commit to becoming green, the conversation and model-building process was successful. Building a good model will not trigger large changes every time but it can raise awareness of a better path of development. In the example above, the board members could have a good grasp on what "good governance" entails and have a deeper commitment on where they want to lead the company in the future.

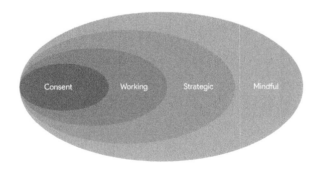

Picture 31: Model of Continuum of Governance

Let's take a look at the parts of the continuum of governance Charlotte Roberts and Martha Summerville designed for the organization.

Consent Board

The tasks of a consent board involve financial supervision, hiring and firing people, understanding customer behavior, compensations, and ethical corporate behavior oversight, among others.

 Senior leaders are responsible for operations and strategy, which the board reviews. The senior leaders give directions to the board, which form the basis of board meetings' agendas, the selection of new board members, and so on. The main decision-maker is the executive committee, yet the issues that get to the board have previously been examined by the CEO and the chair of the board.

There are some downsides to being a consent board for a long time. For example, unpredictable events in the organization can put the board in an awkward position, unethical behavior in the leadership, and boredom can all surface as problems in such a setting.

Working Board

117

Working boards acknowledge that they need to do more than superficial involvement; they need to learn about the organization inside out. This change in board mentality usually happens after a crisis. The structure of a working board usually includes committees such as Finance and Audit, Culture and Employee Engagement, Quality and Safety... Each of these committees has a senior leader assigned to them as a liaison to process important data and assess strategic decisions. To make a working board effective, boundaries must be set and clear responsibility distinction has to be done.

A working board is self-sufficient. They have their own agenda, do evaluation of performance often, and they have face-to-face meetings. Working boards have more responsibilities than consent boards, thus their workload and work hours may be longer.

This form of governance has its own weaknesses, such as becoming comfortable and stagnant in the organizational identity and getting burned out.

Strategic Board

When relationships strengthen between senior leaders and the board, they may evolve to become a strategic board. This usually happens when the board has developed confidence in the skills and aptitude of senior leaders to fulfill their tasks with excellence. Senior leaders are entrusted to develop three- to five-year plans.

When we talk about a strategic board within an organization, board members are actually less involved in the operational tasks. They'd rather focus on the organization's future vision, sustainability, and survivability. The members become genuinely invested in the stewardship mentality and they place high care on the assets of stakeholders, local communities, and the overall society. They shift their organizational framework from operations to sustainability. They have a strong and closely bonded team spirit and are genuinely dedicated to the organization. New hires go through a much more rigorous scanning to make sure they fit into the organization's culture, level of commitment to certain values beyond their general knowledge, skillfulness, and ability to be a team player.

The threats in a strategic board setting may be the inability to reach common ground, and senior leaders may be feeling disenfranchised due to shared decision-making processes.

Mindful Board

When a board becomes involved and concerned about local communities and society is when they might shift towards the mindful governance stage. A mindful board is aware that they have responsibilities beyond financial gain. It is open to innovation, adopting new structures, and even reinventing the organization's core culture and values if needed.

Members look at the organization as being their family, and they take a responsible role in cultivating the organization's values and encouraging quality relationships among main stakeholders. They are aware that the organization is part of a larger system, and that whatever decision the organization makes will have an impact on other elements of the system. Mindful board members have a strong sense of duty and purpose—they are building a better world. They take the questions "Why does this organization deserve to operate for the next century? How will it contribute to the common good? What must we put in place (structure, values, culture, relationships, etc.) to support that purpose?" seriously.

The board members work together with multiple groups within the organization to foster creative thinking and a wide range of solutions.

How to make the transition among the levels of operation.

Let's imagine a company called Patriarchilia. Its board members are all male, the average age is 60, and they are all white—even though this company creates products for young women. The board's president is the one who selects the topics of discussions at board meetings. He has a clear outcome in his mind already, which he pushes down everybody's throats. This system is led by a consummate consent board.

Then a scandal hits Patriarchilia. The president turns out to have an illegitimate child, and he was caught threatening the mother that if she speaks, she and her son will suffer severe consequences. The juicy story is out, the president is forced to resign, and due to the commotion and chaos and fear of future events, shareholders start selling their stocks like crazy. The company's stock price starts dropping.

The board is caught by surprise, and as they start putting our fires, they find severe negligence in how the organization was run.

So they turned into a working board. Some of the older members couldn't keep up with the increased workload and unfamiliar tasks, so they resigned. As the chaos seemed to increase, company stocks were sold at an even larger scale, and its price tanked.

Desperate, and in need of a quick solution, members replaced the old, resigned ones with culturally diverse men and women who had been working in the organization for a long time and had a good sense of what was mismanaged before. Over several years of close and hard work, the organization was saved. Stock prices started rising again as people regained trust in Patriarchilia— which got a new name, Equalitilia.

Trying to learn from previous mistakes, the working board recognized that they were over-managing the organization and that they needed to outsource some operations to committees. So they slowly tapped into becoming a strategic board. This process was not smooth, as the board and the newly formed executive team often locked horns over who had the main work in strategies. Luckily, they managed to meet in the middle with the CEO and its committee focusing on annual and three-year strategies, and board members working on long-term, five-, ten-year planning.

As the board started thinking about the organization's long-term future and sustainability, the questions of fundraisings for charitable causes and environment preservation came up more and more often. They noticed a quality shift in their conversation. It was much more different than in the times of Patriarchilia. While board members were excited about their vision for a greener future for the organization, after long talks with the executive committee and CFO they had to accept that this vision was implementable in 20 years at best, not five. Yet they consulted regularly about what they can do today to reach the desired company structure and culture in 20 years. This deliberate and conscious planning to serve a higher purpose is the sign of a mindful board.

Working on a shared, common goal strengthened the bond between the board and the executive committee. Both became more committed to the organization and each other as they were bound by a shared value and goal.

When the institution has a vision and shared values, the members can start discussing what they need to do to act as stewards for the organization. This is where shared mental models come into the picture. The organization as a collective consciousness starts to discuss past experiences, possible threats, problems that need fixing, and puts them into a mental model in order to have clarity on what they need to change to get to the desired future. Working with shared mental models can accelerate the change process. Having everyone contribute to the common goal fosters bonds, and creates a satisfying work environment.

Here are some tips for getting started in your organization:

- **"Practice together over time.** Hold regular meetings with the same team in which you practice these skills while trying to get to the bottom of the mental models that have created chronic business problems.

- **Prepare for dealing with strong emotions.** When the assumptions behind your models are exposed, you will be chagrined to discover that your actions (or those of your team or organization) are based on erroneous data or incomplete assumptions. Feelings such as anger, embarrassment, or uncertainty may come to the surface. Set time aside for skillful discussion about the emotions that have been raised.

- **Use frustration as a source of new inquiry.** Teams often struggle in mental models work, even when it's oriented to a business problem. Establish an atmosphere in which team members can bring up frustrations for inquiry.

- **Beware of excitement and unbridled action.** When team members break through the limitations they have put on themselves and feel they can at last see the truth about themselves, their work, or their customers, they will be tempted to act immediately. Take the time to pause, reflect on strategy, and design small experiments."[xxvii]

Chapter 5: How to Design Shared Mental Models

Building individual mental models is only the first step in helping organization-wide learning. There are many perceptions of reality within a complex scenario, so evolving the individual mental model into a shared mental model is very important to include the different points of view. Let's take a look at our example from the previous chapter, the ER hospital organization from the perspective of how a group perceives their individual experiences being part of a bigger system.

a.) Construct an integrated map.

Building a shared mental model starts with integrating individual stories into one map. Multiple causal loop diagrams are joined to tell the complete story capturing the main problem clearly. For example, the hospital's residents assigned to the research program had difficulty implementing the new tasks into their regular routines.

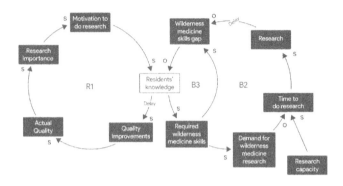

Picture 32: Research–Time Capacity Story

The initial research assignment is met with curiosity and motivation, thus the motivation grows to do more research (R1). But the time–energy capacity of the residents doesn't keep pace with the demand for research generated by the senior medical board, the time shortage to fulfill both regular ER duties and research duties will continue to grow, and residents will start performing more poorly because of the stress of not being there completely in either task. Being stressed, their concentration capacity decreases, so they deliver their research project even slower. We encounter a limits-to-success archetype here as the research project required more time than what was available.

128

In this part of the story, the main loop is reinforcing loop R1, which shows the hospital's initial implementation attempts. We have the main theme identified. Now we can integrate other stories into the central one.

For example, the attendings (the residents' direct coordinators) believed that the time constraints residents were facing had a negative impact on the quality of their regular ER duties. Their individual diagrams showed that, as research demands increased, the level of wilderness accident intervention skills increased as people had more information on how to treat such patients. This increased the demand for more research, which reduced the time and energy to do their regular tasks. And as they didn't have more rest time, they couldn't meet the rising demand (B2). But as research activities decrease, the required skill gap increases, which will negatively effect ER intervention quality in the case of accidents suffered in the wilderness (B3). The main loop's central story thus is expanded to capture all the key issues of all individual maps.

b.) Decomposition

Integrated mental models can have up to 20 or 30 connecting loops. This level of complexity is hard to analyze. The decomposition step allows us to simplify the model, breaking it down into more transparent sub-parts.

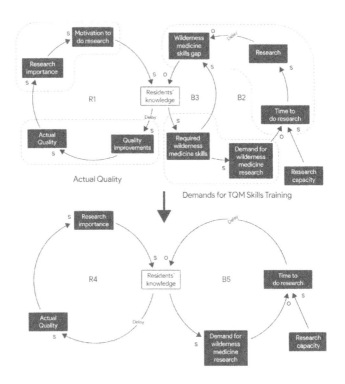

Picture 33: Decomposition

If you take a look at our original map, you can see that many variables can be merged into one. The new, simplified link, however, has to keep the original connection as the complex version.

The next step is identifying the systems archetypes. This step can help a lot in our process of decomposition as it gives a theoretical framework for the story. In the hospital example, the increased research activity is limited by a constraint (time and energy). This observation points to the limits to success archetype. Archetypes are premade stories which can provide us with quick clarity in a confusing and complex problem.

We can't force-fit an archetype to a story. So if we can't detect any archetype, we can decompose the story in another way by finding a relevant behavior pattern. BOT or behavior over time diagrams are very helpful in capturing the dynamic interactions between the elements of the system. In the research capacity story, two behaviors seemed significant: the high demand for research and the time limit to do quality research. Identifying such behavior patterns can help us simplify our mental model while keeping the important dynamics.

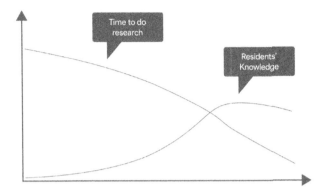

Picture 34: BOT Diagram of the Resident's Research Capacity

As you can see in Picture 34, research activities grow for a while and then start decreasing as the time and energy to do research decreases. This type of behavior is often present in limits-to-success dynamics.

Our complex mental model has only three feedback loops: R1, B2, and B3. But it has 11 variables which can be simplified. When we intend to reduce the number of variables and thus links, we need to be certain that the new variable keeps the original meaning and direction of the old variables. In other words, S (same direction) relationships can't turn into Os, and vice versa.

For example, if we combine the variables "required wilderness medicine skills" and "demand for wilderness medicine research" into a single variable, "demand for wilderness medicine research" goes away because the research skill requirement is not as important as the demand it generates. The net impact to "time to do research" is preserved by an O link.

The last step to do a proper decomposition is to double-check each link and variable and make sure that the loops' quality is still the same. In other words, balancing loops didn't turn into reinforcing ones and vice versa.

Once you're sure your loops have been properly decomposed, it's time to share the new version with the people involved in the system you analyzed. Every party involved in the initial interviews and essential key people in the system should also double-check the simplified mental model to make sure the diagrams represent reality well enough.

This verification requires two things. The first thing is to see if there's a general agreement about the diagram accurately describing the events. The second thing is to see if there is a general agreement in the solutions suggested in fixing the problem.

All this being said, and even if everyone agrees about the depiction' accuracy of the diagrams, the final map or the solutions suggested might not be "good," or "correct." This process serves only to capture the beliefs of the actors involved based on their current understanding of the problem. This mental model designing process doesn't aim to capture reality. Reality testing requires much more complex tools which can only be made by computer simulations.[xxviii]

Chapter 6: Modeling Soft Variables

"How can we trust our model if we add all the broad estimates of variables that are not so easy to measure?"

This indeed is a tricky question for system dynamics modelers and decision-makers alike. When we talk about finances or business, a miscalculation of a few percentiles can lead to big losses. So it is understandable why people dread including qualitative factors in models. Complexity can lead to the decrease of precision. Error measurement potential thus is essential in modeling.

In business analysis we can use two tools: conceptual models, which are often pen-and-paper-based, or computer simulations, like STELLA. The former modeling may have both quantitative and qualitative variables but they are very standard models, so they rarely form the basis of real analysis. Computer models, however, tend to bury or totally eliminate qualitative factors. This leads to a heavy focus on hard, measurable factors—like cash flow, output-input ratio, and so on. Soft variables, as we discussed earlier in this book are intangible things such as work morale, effective problem-solving capacity, employee satisfaction level... Even though they are intangible, soft variables are an important part of the system and they can have a strong influence on it. One important task in understanding dynamic systems which have social aspects is to develop measurement methods for qualitative variables.

Aiming for perfection is not a realistic expectation in this case. There is always a chance for some error in any measurement. Errors can happen even when we have clear units of measurement like cups, watts, or kilograms. Soft variables don't have clear measurement units, so in their case measurement error can happen for two reasons: the definition of a unit of measurement or the creation of the measurement tool.

Let's say we want to measure employee commitment to the organization, so we invent a unit of measure called the employee commitment index. We can create questionnaires, interviews, focus groups, or other tools to measure this new unit. We can come up with a number which would give a good estimate of what employee commitment is at the moment, what would be ideal, and so on.

We need to take into account that both of these steps are prone to error. This warning pushes many people to leave qualitative variables out from computer modeling. Yet, just because soft variables are more prone to measurement error than their hard peers, we should not leave them out. A model's utility and how well it represents the system depends on much more than measurement precision only. Leaving out soft variables might mean missing out on significant feedback loops, and creating an error in presenting dynamic. When we make measurement errors, they are usually local errors—they don't affect the measurements in other areas or time periods. A static measurement error thereby leaves a relatively small impact on the system's representation. Errors in dynamic, opposed to measurement errors, build up over time. The model loses its utility quickly.

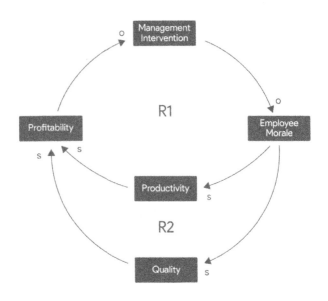

Picture 35: Employee Satisfaction

Take a look at the soft variable "Employee Morale." Management involvement grows as profitability decreases. As an involuntary reaction against the increased management control, employee satisfaction and morale drop. This leads to the employees being less productive, their work quality goes south, and so does profitability. If we don't include this variable, the model will miss a crucial reinforcing element, which will result in a useless model.

Although we can't measure employee satisfaction, its role in the process is indisputable. Even though it can raise worries to include soft variables, leaving them out creates errors in our models.

Let's see how we can add qualitative variables into our computer models. In practice, qualitative variables are added to computer programs by an experienced management team who, by reflecting on previous data, will give a rough estimate of the system's situation. These estimates usually are quite accurate and represent the mental models of the managers in the model building.

The best way to include qualitative variables in a model is to design an indexed variable. We start by setting the value of the variable equal to "1" at some point in time—usually at the beginning of the analysis. Then we can add other variables that will influence our index variable and come up with mathematical calculations, or graphical representations, to illustrate how the indexed variable changes over time.

For example, let's say we generate an index for employee morale, adding "1" as its starting value. We don't make a judgment about the current morale. We don't qualify "1" as being high or low. We just create a starting point.

Then we determine that the ratio of employees to finish all their daily tasks at a high quality and do some extra work within their regular work hours is a key driver of their morale. Third, we need to check—ceteris paribus—what ratio would uphold employee morale at "1," and what would be the consequences if this ratio changed.

For example, we're measuring customer service employee morale. If in their case the "1" state would be 100 emails answered per day, if that number dropped to 60 that would mean there was a 40% drop in customer service employees' work morale. This number, of course, changes over time. So when we run a model we can know with more clarity when work morale raises, drops, oscillates, or stays steady. We can calculate this given the value relative to "1." We could experience, for example, that after a team-building or company excursion, employee morale increases. After a hard year-closing period, it decreases. We can fine-tune our business agenda thanks to this data.

Assessing models.

The best way to present a model to your superiors is to design it both ways: the traditional way, where you don't include soft variables, and in a new way that captures the effect of qualitative variables.

You can try to use both models at the same time, exploring the thinking patterns and assumptions that each include. Use the information to find new insights about the system.

You can try to sway your management team to use modeling as a way to test new ideas and learn about the system instead of a forecasting method. If you are the manager, you need to ask hard questions about the assumptions identified in the models—especially about the soft variables. For example, ask if the identified decrease in employee satisfaction and morale and all its consequences are taken care of in the business plan of the next quarter. Yes? No? Why?

Make sure to end the rule of pure quantitative measurements in your organization. While charts and spreadsheets have their own use, to think about problems in a holistic way you and your team has to learn how to include soft variables in their problem-solving.[xxix]

Chapter 7: Facilitative Modeling

Our world has never been more interconnected than today. This fact makes it harder to understand, and cause-effect relationships are not that obvious. For example, did the war in Iraq or Afghanistan achieve the desired outcome? Why didn't anyone predict and take action before the financial crisis of 2008 hit the world? When we're facing situations of such magnitude, after analyzing them we may end up with more questions than answers.

We don't need to think about global systems to find complexity. Just think about a business organization in your vicinity. They have to analyze and comprehend so many options and choices that they may feel confused where to even begin.

- Should they build a strong HR team or should they invest in research and development first?
- How costly and how rigorous of employee training should they invest in?

- Should they invest in developing new products or promote the existing ones more to increase revenue?

When a company has so many competing needs and each area tries to maximize its own share of the funds, it may backfire and decrease the company's revenue while attempting to increase it. We can't fix every demand at the same time or we'll face chaos. It's more ideal to look for bottleneck issues and start working on those. A bottleneck issue is the problem with the greatest constraint, urgency, or positive impact if fixed. Once we deal with that issue, we can go find the next bottleneck, and so on.

How do you find these bottleneck issues? Using mental models, of course.

How do organizations usually make decisions?

As we could see, optimal organization management is a complex task. What usually happens in a decision-making setting is the following: people get together in team meetings, some people express their ideas—but most employees are silent. Then the manager adds their opinion which everybody agrees with. Done. A decision has been made. This process lacks honesty, as quite often employees criticize the manager's decisions in private. They are not supportive of the decision, so if it even gets implemented, this new decision doesn't take any roots and the organization doesn't experience any positive changes. These kinds of managerial decisions lack two important aspects: support and analytical rigor. It's common knowledge in organizations that managerial decisions have these weaknesses, so they try to bridge the gaps with the following approaches:

1. **The analytical approach**.

The manager, with the hope of increasing analytical rigor, discusses the possible decision with analysts, who use different computerized tools to evaluate the decision. Using pure data analysis may result in lots of numbers and charts, but these by themselves are not enough to fully capture the system's dynamics and come up with an ideal solution.

Organizations who rely on data alone believe that answers are found in numbers.

The charts and statistical spreadsheets are not easily comparable with the decision-maker's own mental models and assumptions. So they may distrust the analysis and may choose to give solution recommendations based on their own mental models, disregarding the charts. This is why the analytical approach rarely results in effective decisions.

2. The support approach.

This approach doesn't rely on technology but rather on the knowledge and support of those involved in the process, the stakeholders. They are holding dialogues, use mental models, and use systems archetypes. This approach relies on representing every player in the system so the situation will be presented in a broader perspective. The stakeholders will feel safe in expressing their genuine opinion, so the outcome may be more creative and systemic.

Picture 36: Approaches for Systems Thinking Implementation

146

Take a look at the picture above. Whenever stakeholders try to define a problem or find solutions, their thinking happens somewhere along the line above. There is an open, a narrow, and a closing phase in decision-making. In the open stage, people gather as much data as possible and define the problem. If they also go for solution creation, this is the stage where creative, wide-perspective suggestions pop up.

Then comes the narrowing phase when stakeholders go through the list of solution options and narrow it down to only a few that are worthy of serious further consideration.

In the closing phase, after modeling and simulating the solutions, stakeholders choose which main problem to address or solution to use. Then each major task is assigned to sub groups to implement. The support approach—as its name suggests—builds much broader and deeper connection and understanding. Those involved will see the system in a much clearer light, and thus the outcomes of decisions made with the support approach tend to lead to more meaningful changes.

The shortcoming of this approach is its narrowing phase. Why? Because whatever people pick from the pool of solutions usually relies on the assumption that if enough people want something, it must be the best choice. This, of course, is not always the case. Barry Richmond, a systems thinking expert, created an exercise that illustrates how many people can guess a (much simpler) system's future behavior. The result was 10-15%. Trusting the assumption that collective decision-making will lead to better results, thus, is flawed.

Also, simply choosing from a large pool of solutions won't tell how, when, and to what degree these solutions should be implemented. The support approach also fails to show if the problems or solutions identified in the narrowing phase are interconnected or mutually exclusive.

Neither does this approach tell you how many resources each solution would demand; it lacks numbers and deep analysis, in other words. Organizations end up investing the same amount of resources into each solution. This may lead to suboptimal results.

Facilitative Modeling

"How can we make good decisions, then?" you may ask. There is a way.

Systems thinkers developed a method that incorporates both the analytical approach and the support approach. While people generally want to learn to think in systems because it's known that it provides a holistic view of problems and, if utilized well, brings everyone on the same page, decision-makers can still get lost in an either-or manner of thinking when it comes to using the analytical method (simulations and charts made by experts) or the support approach (common brainstorming sessions using systems archetypes and mental models).

There is an in-between phase for these two approaches that systems thinkers call "Facilitative Modeling." (Take a look at Picture 36.) This is the zone where true systems thinking happens. It combines the analytical approach—as it uses computer simulations and the scientific method—with the support approach—as it brings stakeholders to the conversation table to create simple models together and explore a broader scale of opinions. These simple models focus on encouraging constructive discussions instead of trying to find solutions.

Facilitative modeling, at its peak, generates common understanding among stakeholders based on combining assumptions and data in conversations, and results in more well-informed decisions.

The process of facilitative modeling.
In the facilitative modeling process, stakeholders detect and talk about a problem crucial to the success of the organization. This problem is often a stubborn one which has proven resistant to previous efforts to solve it.

After deciding on the focal point for examination, the stakeholders set the agenda for a meeting. Several members form a modeling team and create a few simple systems thinking mental models to clearly illustrate the components of the problem. These components might present the history of the problem, possible future consequences if the problem goes on, intervention plans, and the unintended consequences of them. The models should be kept simple so everyone can understand and follow them.

Models by themselves are not enough in the case of facilitative modeling. To have a successful brainstorming session, stakeholders need to add other people to the modelers to create workbooks to track the experiments, create auxiliary materials for the sessions, ask critical questions, suggest tests to run on the model, and have further discussions.

Teams of two to four people should test and examine the models on computers, and at the end of the session, all small groups should unite and discuss their findings.

These are the steps of facilitative modeling:

- "Identify an issue of importance.
- Determine stakeholders who have impact on/from the issue.
- Use stakeholders to redefine the issue (either individually or collectively).
- Develop an agenda for a facilitated session.
- Develop (usually more than one) a model that surfaces important aspects of the issue.
- Develop supporting materials.
- Participate in a session using the models as tools for helping stakeholders explore, experiment with, and discuss the issues.

- Use insights from the models and discussion to determine action items and the next steps based on the insights that emerged during the event."[xxx]

How to use facilitative modeling.

Let's recall our little organization from the last chapter, Equalitilia, which adopted a mindful governance type. They recently discovered some problems related to new funding policy implementations. They were supposed to aid the health of those in need by giving funds to some nonprofit healthcare providers. Equalitilia chose which nonprofits to fund with how much money by examining the services this nonprofit would facilitate. However, in the past few years, instead of making this rigorous examination, Equalitilia has just settled on increasing funding each year. To improve the effectiveness of their funding and create accountability, Equalitilia decided that from this year onwards they would distribute funding based on performance. Meaning, they will estimate what improvements they expect to happen thanks to their funding, and based on how much of these expectations were met, they will calculate next year's funding.

Not everyone was in agreement on the board with the changes. They were concerned about the unintended consequences such changes would create. The board generally agreed that using a facilitative model would bring forth the best-shared insights. The organization, bringing all stakeholders to the table, initiated a brainstorming session.

The group set some rules to guide their interactions and then jumped into analyzing the first model. The goal of the analysis was to detect and talk about possible dynamics related to the implementation of the new funding policy. As we discussed in the previous chapter, the big group of stakeholders broke down into smaller, two-to-four member groups to work with the models at their own pace. This helped them to understand the models better as they didn't feel rushed or left behind.

Reading stock-and-flow diagrams can be tiring even to those who are well practiced in it.

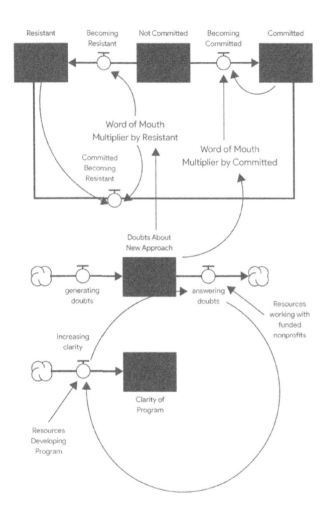

Picture 37: The First Map

The map in Picture 37 illustrates a potential way to look at the different nonprofits affected by

154

Equalitilia's new funding policy. The three stocks at the top of the model—resistant, not committed, and committed—stand for groups of people on Equalitilia's board. Because the new approach was not implemented yet, the entire board would belong to the not-committed stock. As the new funding plan is turned into a policy, board members may migrate to the resistant and committed groups. Of course, the ideal outcome would be if every board member ends up committed.

At the beginning of the session, the small groups had a talk about what each stock meant to them. Who's committed or resistant? How many board members would we need to commit to the new policy to implement it smoothly? Is it possible that committed members change their minds over time? What about resistant members?

With the help of the diagram, the small groups—and later, the big group—arrived to a common conclusion about how some board members might become committed or resistant to the policy change. This was the first time when the topic of resistance even came up. Now they took into consideration that some board members would resist changes. Using the model, the brainstorming group was able to detect this uncomfortable aspect of change in a way that helped them address its implications.

Then they discussed how much time and effort they should invest in the new performance-driven funding policy and in presenting it to the funded nonprofits. How much should they do each of these two tasks before and after officially announcing the changes? In other words, they were discussing the size and time cost needed to successfully execute the policy.

The board agreed that the most urgent thing to develop was the actual design of the new policy. This would offer clarity about the program and would be helpful in impeding any doubts about the new approach. They also agreed that they should involve some of their clients, some representatives from the nonprofits, so they could ask questions about the upcoming change. Having an open dialogue with all stakeholders would help design the most urgent thing, the policy itself, better.

Step two would need some extra work from other stakeholders. This would be the phase when Equalitilia explains the program in detail before it gets released. The last two phases would be about implementation, mainly about the addressing of any doubts from the side of the affected

156

nonprofits. The group concluded that their strategic resource allocation may change over time based on which step they are at. For example, in step two, where they explain the program in detail, they might need to add some extra resources to program development as they expect an increased amount of work with the stakeholders.

Working with mental models.

In facilitative modeling, every model builds on the previous one, broadening understanding. The performance-based funding policy Equalitilia wants to introduce needs a special computer system that would follow up on the development of medical aid systems facilitated by the nonprofits. Based on this data, Equalitilia would renew the funding each year. But this means that each involved nonprofit needs to finance this computer system and train some of their employees to use it.

The need for financing the new computer system asks for another model, namely one that explores how the nonprofit clients could allocate or regroup their resources across these demands: medical care service providing, building and running the computer system, and investment in training some employees to use the computer system.

During the experimenting with the model, an interesting dynamic surfaced. After the change in the funding system, the sense of connection to the community decreased within the young population. At least initially. There was a dip in the general mood right after the changes got implemented—we're talking about simulations still. It didn't matter how the board approached the simulated policy changes, how encouraging and helpful they were with the nonprofits implementing the performance-based policy, the dip kept surfacing. The board leader tried hard to avoid the dip scenario. He was expecting the dip behavior to surface, yet he was stuck in wishful-thinking mode, hoping there was a way it wouldn't.

This discovery was followed with an invigorating talk on a topic that often is considered to be taboo, namely that social system improvement efforts usually need time to bring net positive changes, and that in the initial phases of implementations there is often degradation in efficiency. The board leader feared that if this dip became common knowledge, nobody would subscribe to changes like the performance-based policy, which may lead to long-term benefits but at a short-term cost. Eventually, due to deep conversations with the stakeholders, it became clear that such dynamics may happen—they are almost inevitable as there is a natural delay before computer programs are developed and specialized employees become secure in their skills handling the program. Once this temporary negative consequence of change is accepted and embraced, the brainstorming group can allocate their resources to explore fixes that would alleviate the negative impact of the dip.

Overall, the discussion brought new insights to the surface:

- Equalitilia's board understood that some of the nonprofits may resist the new policies.
- They also realized that it would be beneficial for everyone if the representatives of these nonprofits would get a seat at the discussion/policy development table.
- They also figured that training specialized employees to handle the computer program designed for the new policy will be more challenging and time demanding than the computer program itself.
- Last but not least, the system-level implementation of the new policy would create an

initial dip in performance before it starts delivering the desired results.

The example of Equalitilia shows that small models can have a huge impact in systems mapping. Facilitative modeling applies the best of both the analytical approach and the support approach, creating a facilitated environment where people think in systems to find the best solutions for everyone. Plus, facilitative modeling uses layman-friendly language through simple stock and flow models, ensuring that all participants will be able to follow the discussion. Running tests and simulations on the model brings new understanding and provides further topics of conversation about possible alternative outcomes. Facilitative modeling creates a safe space for discussions.[xxxi]

Chapter 8: From Blame to Accountability[xxxii]

What's the first question you ask when something goes wrong? "Whose fault is this?" Right? When a client is lost, it is customer support's fault. When a promotion is unsuccessful, it is the marketing team's fault.

Mistakes made either within a company or in one's personal life seems to attract scapegoat searching. Even people with a growth mindset can fall prey to this trap, naming and blaming the person at fault. Once it's identified, and we also find out what's wrong with this person, we get peace of mind that we traced down the problem. Obviously, it's because of them why things went wrong, and the solution, obviously, is to get rid of them. Right? Isn't this a general way of looking at a problem? It's a human thing to do.

This common behavior pattern prevents us from an important aspect of improvement—blame deprives us of learning; there is no open mindedness or understanding of issues on a system level. Another harmful byproduct of a blaming environment is dishonesty. People who make mistakes, afraid of being blamed and other negative consequences, stop taking responsibility and try to cover up their mistakes and mask important problems. If this chain of behavior is a regular tendency at an organization, sooner or later productivity will start to decrease, ghost problems start to arise, and no one will know from where. The information flow is fake, thus decision-making and problem-solving—if there is any—is ineffective, as the real problems don't get fixed.

Blaming in this sense can cost resources, money, and in a severe case, even our business. When people are tense, finger pointing at each other, that's where their focus will go—not in making the business more successful. They will not work on product development, promotion opportunities, and mapping revenue-increasing options. All they will care about is to look blameless, and hopefully the other person will seem at fault.

How can we avoid creating a blame-heavy company culture? There are a few steps.

Clarifying accountability.

Being specific about who is responsible for what in advance is the first step to creating a culture of accountability.   Accountability-based conversations will help people get accustomed to openness about problems and will help in the verification of a common understanding. Clear contracting is also essential to make sure tasks are accomplished, standards met, and expected results delivered.

Being accountable doesn't equal being the one to be blamed. Many people tend to use these two terms as synonyms—that's why they cringe upon hearing of accountability or responsibility. Being accountable, as a term defined by the dictionary, is "to be counted on or reckoned on." Blaming, on the other hand, is defined as "finding fault with, to censure, revile, reproach." Clearly different meanings. Accountability encourages the keeping of agreements in a safe space; blaming is discrediting someone in a toxic environment.

Accountability doesn't exclude the possibility of errors happening; everyone can make mistakes. But when we are held accountable and we take responsibility for our shortcomings, we can learn from our mistakes, grow from there, and do better in the future. Accountability is the tool for constructive conversations and awareness of the present reality. Being aware of the real problems, we can understand the system better and design solutions from a more authentic place. The main qualities accountability relies on are trust, respect, honesty, curiosity, authenticity, and mutuality.

Blaming, in contrast, is a shaming tool—seeking the fault in someone and pointing it out even in public. It only provides superficial and simplistic treatment to a symptom of a complex problem. "I know you're the problem." This approach makes respect, trust, authenticity, and curiosity difficult. It also sabotages the chance to find the real problem. People get fearful if they are blamed too often; they may feel that they are considered bad or unskillful. Blame attracts reactions such as anger, fear, judgment, sense of inadequacy, and entitlement.

The consequences of blame.

As we discussed before, blame tilts or slows down information flow and reduces productivity. Some people use blame to make others take responsibility for problems. This is a bad strategy, though, because people will start to link errors and bad news with retribution. This chain of events sets up two reinforcing loops:

- Managers who demand information yet punish if they get bad news.
- Employees who will cover information up either to protect themselves or to blame each other.

Who doesn't work doesn't have mistakes in their job, they say. And who works, makes mistakes, and doesn't admit it, won't learn.

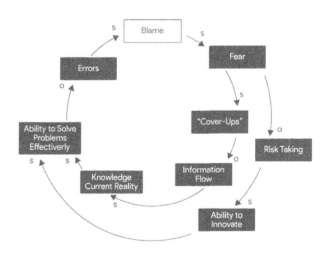

Picture 38: The Reinforcing Cycles of Blame

Picture 38 shows how blame leads to fear. Fear leads to cover-ups, which cause a slowdown in the information flow and develops a lack in current knowledge. In these conditions, effective problem-solving becomes a challenge, which naturally leads to errors. And as we know, someone must be blamed for those errors. The first reinforcing loop (R1) is complete and in action.

What happens next is even more discouraging. The fear of being blamed reduces creative thinking. People who are afraid won't take risks. Innovation and risk go hand in hand. If there is no innovation, effective problem-solving is, again, lacking—thus, errors will happen (R2).

Blame as a systems archetype.

Blaming creates an archetypical cycle, namely "shifting the burden." As we saw, people tend to find easy, quick fixes instead of digging deeper into problems. This creates a vicious cycle of repeated quick fixes and the core problem resurfaces over and over again. Blame is such a quick fix.

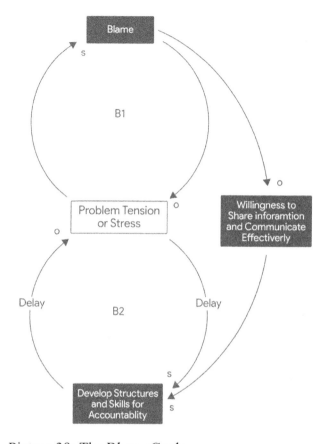

Picture 39: The Blame Cycle

Blame shifts attention from real, long-term,
system-level solutions (see B1). While blame
might give short-term gratification and the false
hope that the problem has been dealt with, it
drives focus away from accountability even more
(B2) and destroys constructive communication

and the willingness to share honest information (R3), which drives people further away from developing a structure of accountability (B2).

Blame has a psychological aspect to it as well. People who blame usually feel they have the upper hand, that they are more powerful. They also become blind to their own shortcomings. For example, Mike was up all night to help out Doug with an urgent project. He delivered the project on time but he made a design error which Doug was reprimanded for by his superiors. Doug called up Mike angrily, saying his work was of poor quality. Mike, feeling unappreciated and attacked, blamed Doug for not starting his project in the first place and being very critical. If they don't dig deeper into the issue, both can walk away offended, thinking they were right. Doug feels entitled for his anger as Mike's design error caused him to look bad in front of his bosses. Mike could also feel rightfully resentful as he sacrificed his date night to help a friend out with a project that was not even his job, yet all he received was criticism.

How can we move from blame to accountability?

Errors can happen even in the best-designed systems. And even with a clear vision on systems dynamics we can still look at individual mistakes as root causes of problems. One way to change the blame dynamic is to understand the two vicious reinforcing loops it creates. Another way is to intentionally change our attitude at work.

Marilyn Paul, a systems thinking expert, distinguishes between three levels of behavioral change in shifting from blame to accountability: the individual, the interpersonal, and the organizational levels.

Individual Level

In order to shift from blame to accountability, we need to be familiar with both of them. Awareness is the first step in changing our mental models about blame. When you feel the urge to blame someone, take a step back and think about what your goal is with blaming. You want to solve the problem, right? By now, we know that whatever the problem is, blame is not the solution.

1. **Keep in mind that people rarely have intentions, and from their perspective, their actions might be rational.** Taking into consideration their current knowledge, the

pressures they may be under, and expectations on them, they may be doing the best they can. Don't rush into giving someone a bad name.

2. **Look for your role in the problem.** Maybe you are frightening, too insistent; your behavior might influence the behavior of the other person. Also, you may be justifying your own point of view at the cost of the other person's.

3. **Remember that being judgmental and critical are not traits of the open-minded.** Without an open mind, you can't take in new data, and learning new things is challenging, too. Judgmental people can get angry quicker. Let's see what you can do when you're seeing red:

- What am I missing that prevents me from understanding this person?
- Can their behavior make sense?
- Are they facing uncertainty or pressure?
- Is there a systemic structure creating the behavior I dislike?

4. **Systems thinking can help you walk a bit in the other person's shoes and see what pressures they are facing.** There is always a bigger influencing force that controls the behavior of people.

For example, if the economy is bad and someone's losing money, they might make rushed, irrational decisions, trying to stay afloat like a drowning man. Also, if in a company there are no clear values and assigned responsibilities, people might work toward conflicting goals. When a situation is tense, try to analyze the interconnections between the elements involved, or even try to see if you can identify a systems archetype. Accidental adversaries or shifting the burden are typical systems archetypes that can affect an organization.

5. **Take responsibility and be accountable.** This means that you are investigating your own actions and trying to find out the answer to the following questions:

- What's my role in this problem?
- Did I take actions that backfired—even if at the time they seemed like a good idea?

6. **Be self-reflective.** Try to discover what underlying problems you have that you are masking with anger. In a healthy work environment, conflict and tension can also be a great personal growth opportunity:

- What did I discover about myself thanks to this problem?
- Is my behavior something that I learned from someone? Who? How did this behavior affect their lives? Do I want to change?
- What qualities do I need to improve in myself?

Interpersonal Level

When we start working together with someone, it's very important to set some ground rules about the purpose of the work, clear tasks, deadlines, expectations, action methods, milestones, and roles. Similarly, it's good to have a discussion about how to approach conflict, miscommunication, or failure in advance. Having clear expectations and designed conflict resolution processes ready can help everyone be more prepared and relaxed. When a conflict arises or mistakes are made, they need to be handled non-judgmentally, collectively, and quickly—before anger and blame occur. Hard feelings unaddressed will just fester and escalate. But if they are dealt with in a timely manner, things can get better faster.

Accountability Conversations

Having accountability conversations periodically is a great way to check if people are still on the same page. It's good to repeat the expectations, tasks, roles, and standards of the organization over time. The more people hear them, the more they will memorize and act in accordance with them. This conversation is also useful to check which values are easy to follow and which are not working. New strategies can be developed for the parts that are not working.

This being said, accountability conversations can be difficult. But if led skillfully, using inquiry instead of inquisition, listening instead of attacking, these conversations are productive and honest.

How to lead an accountability conversation:

1. **First, explore if the person you want to talk with has a learning mindset.** If yes, when an issue happens, include some outsiders in the conversation who can provide helpful feedback and who have a deep understanding and broader perspective about the problem. Two people who are in conflict can rarely have the required insight to solve the larger, system-level problem.

2. **Create a learning environment.** Don't rush to address the problem. Make sure to emphasize that no one is there to blame or be ashamed—the purpose of the conversation is to learn. Make sure to treat confidential information as such. Encourage an atmosphere of open-mindedness and be a good listener.

Be clear about what the purpose of the meeting is. Bring forth the data you have and also some assumptions or conclusions about the data. What are the explicit or implicit expectations and agreements that might still not be understood? Bring them to light and clarify them again if needed. Try to find new ways to address the problem.

Group Level

Emotional safety within an organization can affect a lot of people's behavior. If they feel as though they're in a safe space, they accept accountability easier, they trust deeper, and are able to discuss their issues directly instead of going to a third party to seek comfort.

Let's see how the negative example works: Rita was upset that Jane got a promotion even though

Rita worked longer for the firm. Seeing it as injustice, she goes to complain about it to Greg. Greg feels bad for Rita and he agrees she should have got the promotion. Rita's pain is validated and Greg seems like a reasonable colleague, and she wants to build an alliance with him. Another day when Rita wants to share something with Greg, the man doesn't have time due to other obligations. Frustrated, Rita goes to Jane to complain about Greg's lack of support. This dynamic only creates gossip and estranged relationships.

The alternative to this unhealthy communication is to be committed to learn instead of just seeking quick fixes for a bad mood. Rita could have gone to her boss and asked her directly why Jane got the promotion.

The answer might have been painful, but would have given Rita an idea where to improve. Greg could have sympathized with Rita but also tell her that he is very impressed with Jane's work ethic and problem-solving skills. Greg could have also indicated that Rita should talk things through with Jane.

How to resolve conflicts.

1. When you are facing a conflict with someone, it is good to bring in a moderator—a coach who you trust—and include them in the conflict resolution. The coach will ask you about the situation; both of you should present your perspective, trying to stay away from blame.

Then you should discuss what outcome you expect from the conversation. A good coach will lead you to try to empathize with the other person's perspective and encourage you to explain the other person's actions and motivations differently than how you experienced them. For example, what if he just had a bad day and that's why he cut you short in your story, not because he doesn't care?

Both of the involved parties should practice some coordinated self-reflection then and try to find their own contributions to the problem. Are there any requests each of the involved parties would like to share with the other? How can one phrase these requests to get to the desired outcome? What can they both learn in this situation?

2. Make sure to reinforce your desire of maintaining a positive work environment and good relationships. Make sure to be respectful to

176

each other. It's you against the problem, not each other. Bring forth the information that caused the friction or concern. Talk about your assumptions and emotions related to the issue. What change do you wish to happen?

Make sure that the part where you bring in the data is aimed to learn to work together better in the future, not to blame.

3. Ask about the coach's opinion about the problem.

4. Don't bring the conflict resolution conversation's topic outside of the safe space where you had the discussion. Don't gossip. Be trustworthy.

5. If you are the third party and you want to encourage a constructive learning process, don't engage in gossip. Tell the complainer that you'd be more than happy to help them and the person they're in conflict with to solve their problems, but you would prefer not to listen to one side's story only.

When people are well intentioned, and genuinely interested in solving conflicts, they will follow the five steps of discussion presented above.

Final Thoughts

In this book I introduced the key mental models from systems thinking which are essential towards cognitive growth. Mental models are our deeply ingrained and held beliefs, assumptions, generalizations, or abstractions based on our experience. They influence us in how we understand the world, our work, our relationships, and how we take actions.

Often, we are unconsciously aware of our mental models or the effects they have on our behavior. The lack of mental model awareness limits us to familiar ways of thinking only, and robs us of improvement and self-reflection. The practice of managing our mental models, therefore, is very important.

Discovering, experimenting with, and improving our internal beliefs about how the world works promises to be a major breakthrough for building a more mindful and organized life.

A.R.

Reference

Cambridge Dictionary. Non-Linear. Cambridge Dictionary. 2020. https://dictionary.cambridge.org/dictionary/english/non-linear

Cats, Herding. Open Loop Thinking vs. Close Loop Thinking. Herding Cats. 2015. https://herdingcats.typepad.com/my_weblog/2015/03/open-loop-thinking-v-close-loop-thinking.html

Dash, Mike. Critical Thinking. What it is. How it works. Why it matters. Macat. 2012. https://static1.squarespace.com/static/59b7cd299f74569a3aaf0496/t/5afeb67003ce6445740c9563/1526642291284/CT_ebook_Feb_18.pdf

Diagram 17. Original picture from Northwest Earth Institute. A Systems Thinking Model: The Iceberg. Northwest Earth Institute. 2018. https://www.nwei.org/iceberg/

Duke University. Predator-Prey Models. Duke University. 2019.

https://services.math.duke.edu/education/ccp/materials/diffeq/predprey/pred1.html

G. A. Miller . "The Magical Number Seven, Plus or Minus Two: Some Limits on Our Capacity for Processing Information". The Systems Thinker. 1956.

Gerber, John. Systems Thinking Tools: Finding The Root Cause(S) Of Big Problems. Changing The Story. 2012. https://changingthestory.net/2012/07/18/rootcaus/

Hennessy, Greg. Modeling "Soft" Variables. The Systems Thinker. 2020. https://thesystemsthinker.com/modeling-soft-variables/

I See Systems. Applying Systems Thinking and Common Archetypes to Organizational Issues. Module 6: Systems Archetypes. 2018. https://www.iseesystems.com/Online_training/course/module6/6-02-0-0-what.htm

Karash, Richard. Mental Models And Systems Thinking: Going Deeper Into Systemic Issues. The Systems Thinker. 2020. https://thesystemsthinker.com/mental-models-and-systems-thinking-going-deeper-into-systemic-issues/

Kim, Daniel. From Individual To Shared Mental Models. The Systems Thinker. 2020. https://thesystemsthinker.com/from-individual-to-shared-mental-models/

Kim, Daniel. Using Causal Loop Diagrams To Make Mental Models Explicit. The Systems Thinker. 2020. https://thesystemsthinker.com/using-causal-loop-diagrams-to-make-mental-models-explicit/

Merritt, Jeremy. What Are Mental Models? Part 2. The Systems Thinker. 2020. https://thesystemsthinker.com/what-are-mental-models-part-2/

Northwest Earth Institute. A Systems Thinking Model: The Iceberg. Northwest Earth Institute. 2018. https://www.nwei.org/iceberg/

Nunez, Kirsten. 5 Proven Ways Creativity Is Good for Your Health. Verilymag. 2016. https://verilymag.com/2016/01/mental-emotional-health-creativity-happiness

Paul, Marylin. Moving From Blame to Accountability. The Systems Thinker. 2020. https://thesystemsthinker.com/moving-from-blame-to-accountability/

Richmond, Barry. Dynamic Thinking. The Systems Thinker. 2019. https://thesystemsthinker.com/dynamic-thinking-a-behavioral-context/

Richmond, Barry. The "Thinking" In Systems Thinking: How Can We Make It Easier To Master? The Systems Thinker. 2019. https://thesystemsthinker.com/the-thinking-in-systems-thinking-how-can-we-make-it-easier-to-master/

Roberst, Charlotte. Until The Vulcan Mind Meld… Building Shared Mental Models. The Systems Thinker. 2020. https://thesystemsthinker.com/until-the-vulcan-mind-meld-building-shared-mental-models/

Roberts, Charlotte. What You Can Expect… in Working with Mental Models in The Fifth Discipline Fieldbook by Peter M. Senge, Art Kleiner, Charlotte Roberts, Richard B. Ross, and Bryan J. Smith. Doubleday/Currency. 1994.

Soderquist, Chris. Facilitative Modeling: Using Small Models To Generate Big Insights. The Systems Thinker. 2020. https://thesystemsthinker.com/facilitative-modeling-using-small-models-to-generate-big-insights/

Sparks, Chris. 104: Systems Thinking—The Essential Mental Models Needed for Growth. Medium. 2017. https://medium.com/@SparksRemarks/systems-thinking-the-essential-mental-models-needed-for-growth-5d3e7f93b420

Systemic Thinking. The Fractal Phenomemon. Systemic Thinking. 2018. http://systemicthinking.com/the-fractal-phenomenon.html

Endnotes

[i] *Diagram 17*. Original picture from Northwest Earth Institute. A Systems Thinking Model: The Iceberg. Northwest Earth Institute. 2018. https://www.nwei.org/iceberg/

[ii] Gerber, John. Systems Thinking Tools: Finding The Root Cause(S) Of Big Problems. Changing The Story. 2012. https://changingthestory.net/2012/07/18/rootcaus/

[iii] Northwest Earth Institute. A Systems Thinking Model: The Iceberg. Northwest Earth Institute. 2018. https://www.nwei.org/iceberg/

[iv] I See Systems. Applying Systems Thinking and Common Archetypes to Organizational Issues. Module 6: Systems Archetypes. 2018. https://www.iseesystems.com/Online_training/course/module6/6-02-0-0-what.htm

[v] Richmond, Barry. The "Thinking" In Systems Thinking: How Can We Make It Easier To Master? The Systems Thinker. 2019. https://thesystemsthinker.com/the-thinking-in-systems-thinking-how-can-we-make-it-easier-to-master/

[vi] Nunez, Kirsten. 5 Proven Ways Creativity Is Good for Your Health. Verilymag. 2016. https://verilymag.com/2016/01/mental-emotional-health-creativity-happiness

[vii] Systemic Thinking. The Fractal Phenomemon. Systemic Thinking. 2018. http://systemicthinking.com/the-fractal-phenomenon.html

[viii] Dash, Mike. Critical Thinking. What it is. How it works. Why it matters. Macat. 2012. https://static1.squarespace.com/static/59b7cd299f74569a3aaf0496/t/5afeb67003ce6445740c9563/1526642291284/CT_ebook_Feb_18.pdf

[ix] Richmond, Barry. Dynamic Thinking. The Systems Thinker. 2019.

https://thesystemsthinker.com/dynamic-thinking-a-behavioral-context/

[x] Richmond, Barry. The "Thinking" In Systems Thinking: How Can We Make It Easier To Master? The Systems Thinker. 2019. https://thesystemsthinker.com/the-thinking-in-systems-thinking-how-can-we-make-it-easier-to-master/

[xi] Picture 4 extracted from The Systems Thinker. 2019.

[xii] Cats, Herding. Open Loop Thinking vs. Close Loop Thinking. Herding Cats. 2015. https://herdingcats.typepad.com/my_weblog/2015/03/open-loop-thinking-v-close-loop-thinking.html

[xiii] Picture 5 extracted from The Systems Thinker. 2019.

[xiv] Richmond, Barry. The "Thinking" In Systems Thinking: How Can We Make It Easier To Master? The Systems Thinker. 2019. https://thesystemsthinker.com/the-thinking-in-

systems-thinking-how-can-we-make-it-easier-to-master/

[xv] Pictures 6, 7, 8: Extracted from stock photos: https://www.istockphoto.com/il/photo/playing-fetch-with-agile-beagle-dog-gm522369142-91594449, https://www.cairnsattractions.com.au/explore/adventurous-activities/cairns-skydiving.369.html, http://www.noiportal.hu/gyermek/balesetveszely-az-otthonunkban

[xvi] G. A. Miller . "The Magical Number Seven, Plus or Minus Two: Some Limits on Our Capacity for Processing Information". The Systems Thinker. 1956.

[xvii] Cambridge Dictionary. Non-Linear. Cambridge Dictionary. 2020. https://dictionary.cambridge.org/dictionary/english/non-linear

[xviii] Sparks, Chris. 104: Systems Thinking—The Essential Mental Models Needed for Growth. Medium. 2017.

https://medium.com/@SparksRemarks/systems-thinking-the-essential-mental-models-needed-for-growth-5d3e7f93b420

[xix] Sparks, Chris. 104: Systems Thinking—The Essential Mental Models Needed for Growth. Medium. 2017. https://medium.com/@SparksRemarks/systems-thinking-the-essential-mental-models-needed-for-growth-5d3e7f93b420

[xx] Sparks, Chris. 104: Systems Thinking—The Essential Mental Models Needed for Growth. Medium. 2017. https://medium.com/@SparksRemarks/systems-thinking-the-essential-mental-models-needed-for-growth-5d3e7f93b420

[xxi] Duke University. Predator-Prey Models. Duke University. 2019. https://services.math.duke.edu/education/ccp/materials/diffeq/predprey/pred1.html

[xxii] Merritt, Jeremy. What Are Mental Models? Part 2. The Systems Thinker. 2020.

https://thesystemsthinker.com/what-are-mental-models-part-2/

[xxiii] Karash, Richard. Mental Models And Systems Thinking: Going Deeper Into Systemic Issues. The Systems Thinker. 2020. https://thesystemsthinker.com/mental-models-and-systems-thinking-going-deeper-into-systemic-issues/

[xxiv]Kim, Daniel. Using Causal Loop Diagrams To Make Mental Models Explicit. The Systems Thinker. 2020. https://thesystemsthinker.com/using-causal-loop-diagrams-to-make-mental-models-explicit/

[xxv] Picture 28 extracted from The Systems Thinker. 2019.

[xxvi] Roberst, Charlotte. Until The Vulcan Mind Meld… Building Shared Mental Models. The Systems Thinker. 2020. https://thesystemsthinker.com/until-the-vulcan-mind-meld-building-shared-mental-models/

xxvii Roberts, Charlotte. What You Can Expect…
in Working with Mental Models in The Fifth
Discipline Fieldbook by Peter M. Senge, Art
Kleiner, Charlotte Roberts, Richard B. Ross, and
Bryan J. Smith. Doubleday/Currency. 1994.

xxviii Kim, Daniel. From Individual To Shared
Mental Models. The Systems Thinker. 2020.
https://thesystemsthinker.com/from-individual-to-
shared-mental-models/

xxix Hennessy, Greg. Modeling "Soft" Variables.
The Systems Thinker. 2020.
https://thesystemsthinker.com/modeling-soft-
variables/

xxx Soderquist, Chris. Facilitative Modeling: Using
Small Models To Generate Big Insights. The
Systems Thinker. 2020.
https://thesystemsthinker.com/facilitative-
modeling-using-small-models-to-generate-big-
insights/

[xxxi] Soderquist, Chris. Facilitative Modeling: Using Small Models To Generate Big Insights. The Systems Thinker. 2020. https://thesystemsthinker.com/facilitative-modeling-using-small-models-to-generate-big-insights/

[xxxii] Paul, Marylin. Moving From Blame to Accountability. The Systems Thinker. 2020. https://thesystemsthinker.com/moving-from-blame-to-accountability/

Made in United States
North Haven, CT
22 April 2024

51656474R00109